A DICTIONARY OF CRICKET

M A Pervez

Sangam Books

SANGAM BOOKS (INDIA) LIMITED

Registered Office
3-5-820 Hyderguda
Hyderabad 500 029

Distributed by
Orient Longman Limited

Other Offices
Bangalore/Bhopal/Bhubaneshwar/Calcutta/Chandigarh
Chennai/Ernakulam/Guwahati/Hyderabad/Jaipur
Lucknow/Mumbai/New Delhi/Patna

ISBN 81 7370 184 9

Typeset in Aldine 9/11 by
OSDATA
Hyderabad 500 029, India

Illustrated by P Bala Bhakta Raju

Printed in India at
Orion Printers
Hyderabad 500 004

Published by
Sangam Books (India) Ltd.
3-5-820 Hyderguda
Hyderabad 500 029

Contents

FOREWORD

Cricket is probably the only game in the world, which offers so much to so many people. I can say without fear of contradiction that more books have been written about this game than any other in the world because it offers so much to players, administrators and spectators. In terms of statistics it is indeed fascinating and mind-boggling.

Having been associated with the game for more than forty years in various capacities, I thought I knew almost everything there is to know about the game and the terminologies used in it. But, I should admit that was before I had a copy of *A Dictionary of Cricket* in my hands. The author, after years of outstanding research, has brought out a book which should find a prominent place in every cricket follower's collection.

The advent of television coverage and the introduction of one-day cricket has brought about the usage of certain terms which would never have been thought of in the past. Cricket, like the English language, borrows and makes its own, various terms from the many different parts of the world in which it is played.

I am sure that anyone, whether he is a budding cricket player, an enthusiast or an ardent follower of the game would no longer be puzzled by the terms 'Manhattan' or 'Wormgraph', thanks to this *Dictionary*.

M A Pervez has taken pains to explain the terms in simple English. This book would also help coaches teach their pupils to enrich their knowledge of the game and grasp the fundamentals better.

Whenever the need arises, more terms will certainly be added to the book to make it as complete as is humanly possible.

I have no doubt in my mind that this *Dictionary* will be an instant success all over the world.

S Venkataraghavan

Chennai
August 2000

PREFACE

It is sometimes said that cricket is a South Asian game that was invented in England. So great is the game's popularity in the Indian sub-continent that this part of the world now ranks foremost in terms of followers and the amount of cricket played.

In India, cricket has long crossed the borders of cities and towns to reach the people in the remotest of villages. There is now a wave of interest, particularly among the young, not limited merely to knowing the scores of the matches being played, but which goes deeper. Today, many people are conversant with and knowledgeable about the technical aspects of the game and so are able to enjoy it more fully.

However, as both the game and its expressions are complex, there is often difficulty in appreciating the finer aspects of cricket. *A Dictionary of Cricket* brings together, in a user-friendly format, the cricketing words and expressions that constitute the living vocabulary of the game. Although the average user is more than likely to be aware of the basics of the game, the *Dictionary* assumes little or no prior knowledge of it. The terms and expressions are explained as they are applied and followed when cricket is played at any standard level.

The jargon of cricket is so rich and varied that it comprises well over a thousand terms and expressions that are used in playing the game as well as in dealing with its non-playing aspects such as administration, record-keeping and commentating. While many of the terms are unique to cricket (googly, yorker, bouncer, etc.) there are numerous others (cover, slip, third man, etc.) which are a part of the common corpus of English words but which have a special meaning when applied to cricket.

A Dictionary of Cricket includes all these terms and expressions and explains them in clear and simple language, a number of them with illustrations. Also included are many colloquial terms (bosie, zooter, doosra, etc.) which are commonly used in some cricket-playing countries and which make interesting reading.

This *Dictionary* is the outcome of several years of research. I hope that it will serve as a useful aid to all beginners who wish to improve their technical knowledge of the game as well as to the initiated who would like to use it as a source of reference and clarification.

Abbreviations used in Cricket

ACB	Australian Cricket Board
Agg	Aggregate (runs scored)
Avg	Average
b	Bowled
BCCI	Board of Control for Cricket in India
BCCP	Board of Control for Cricket in Pakistan
c	Caught
C	Catches
CCI	Cricket Club of India
c & b	Caught and bowled
cbw	Caught behind the wicket
cap	Captain
CBFS	Cricketers Benefit Fund Series (Sharjah)
D/L	Duckworth–Lewis Formula
dnb	Did not bat
ECB	English Cricket Board
E/R	Economy Rate
F	Fifties
H	Hundreds
ht wkt	Hit Wicket
ICC	International Cricket Council
ing	Innings
IWCC	International Women's Cricket Council
lb	Leg-byes
lbw	Leg before wicket
LHB	Left-hand batsman
LOI	Limited-Overs International
M	Maiden (overs)
MCC	Marleyborne Cricket Club
MCG	Melbourne Cricket Ground
nb	No balls

no	Not out
NRR	Net Run Rate
O	Over
ODI	One-Day International
R	Runs
RHB	Right-hand batsman
RR	Rain Rule/Run Rate
SLCB	Sri Lanka Cricket Board
S/R	Strike Rate
st	Stumped; Stumpings
TCCB	Test and County Cricket Board
UCBSA	United Cricket Board of South Africa
v cap	Vice-captain
W	Wickets; Wide balls
WICB	West Indian Cricket Club
wk	Wicket-keeper
wkt	Wicket

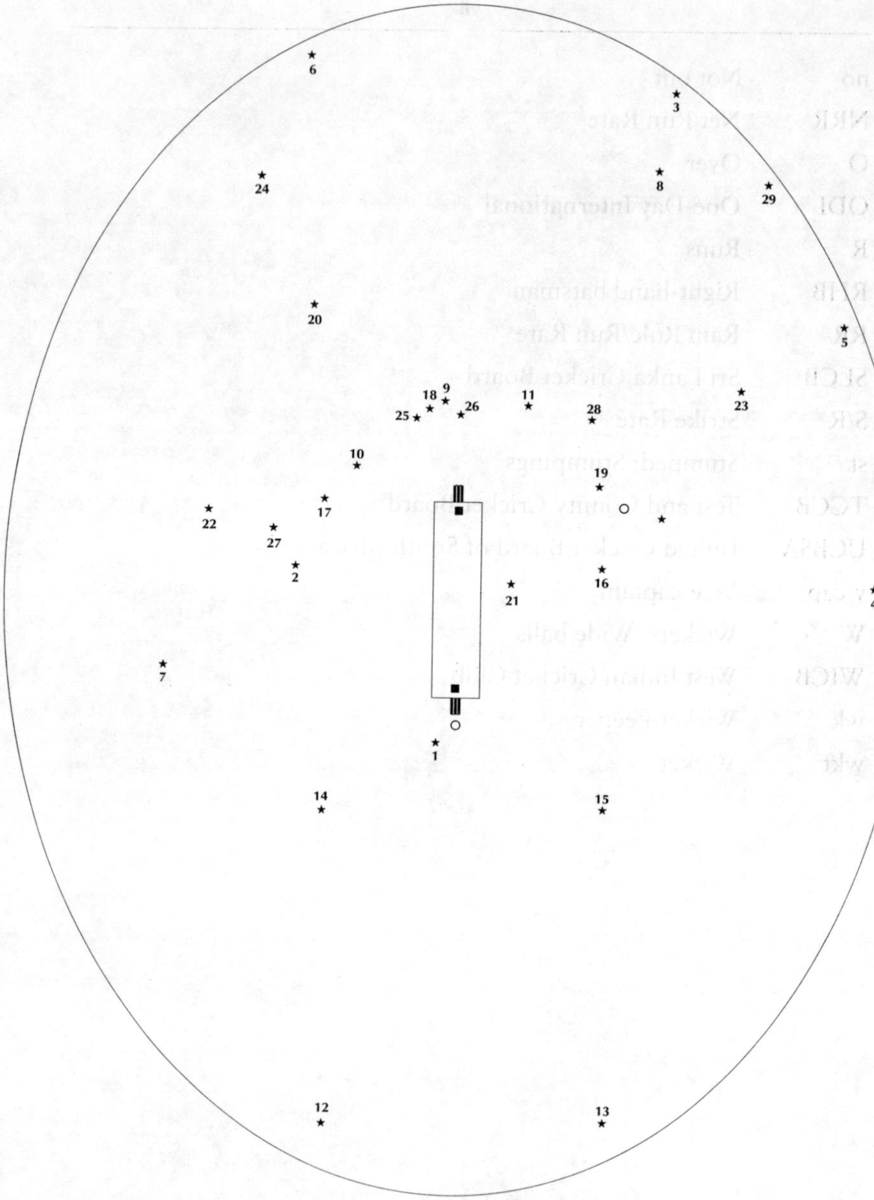

1. Bowler
2. Covers
3. Deep fine leg
4. Deep mid-wicket
5. Deep square leg
6. Deep third man
7. Extra cover
8. Fine leg
9. First slip
10. Gully
11. Leg slip
12. Long off
13. Long on
14. Mid-off
15. Mid-on
16. Mid-wicket
17. Point
18. Second slip
19. Short square leg
20. Short third man
21. Silly mid-on
22. Square cover-point
23. Square leg
24. Third man
25. Third slip
26. Wicket keeper
27. Cover point
28. Leg gully
29. Long Leg

★ Field positions
■ Batsmen
○ Umpires

A a

abdominal guard A small (palm-sized) concave shield, made of plastic, or other hard material, worn inside the trousers to protect the genitals from injury; worn compulsorily by batsmen and wicket-keepers, and sometimes by close-in fielders.

above shoulder height In limited-overs cricket, a delivery passing above the batsman's shoulder is declared a no-ball. This is to discourage negative, or hostile intent of bowling. In first-class matches, such restrictions are less stringent, but still subject to control by the umpires within the specified rules.

accelerate Forceful batting to score runs at a faster pace than normal.

accumulator A batsman who scores his runs patiently, relying on good placements for ones and twos rather than on attacking shots to score runs.

acknowledge Gesture by a batsman e.g. raising his bat, or taking off his cap, in response to the applause from spectators when he reaches a batting milestone, or plays a valuable knock.

acknowledge

across *(1 bowling)* A delivery slanted across the pitch, rather than bowled in a straight line with the wickets. *(2 batting)* To move towards the off-side of the wicket – mostly off the back foot – to play a stroke.

across the line To play a shot with an angled bat, swinging it across the path of delivery, as opposed to playing it with a straight bat. Playing across the line is considered risky due to the lower probability of connecting bat to ball.

action A bowler's individual style of bowling, comprising the run-up, delivery and follow-through.

action break A delivery made to deviate after pitching, by pronounced use of body action and grip.

adjudged out An appeal for dismissal upheld by the umpire after a moment's deliberation, as distinct from a clearly visible and straight-forward dismissal.

aerial route A powerful shot, hitting the ball high up in the air, aiming to lob it into a vacant area, or send it to the ropes.

afternoon session The two hours of play between lunch and tea in a first-class match. In a limited-overs match played to standard day timing, the afternoon session commences after lunch and lasts until the team batting second completes its innings.

aggregate The total number of runs scored over several innings under reference, e.g. a batsman's aggregate in a series, or aggregate runs in a match.

agricultural shot An unorthodox shot that relies on power and robustness, rather than good batting technique. The phrase takes its meaning from countryside cricket, where most players have agricultural backgrounds and tend to play the game in their own rustic style.

aim *(1 batting)* To contemplate a hit in a given direction. *(2 bowling)* To direct a delivery to a particular spot.

air The flight imparted on a delivery by a slow bowler by tossing the ball up so that it remains in the air for a longer time than normal before landing. Spin bowlers often use this technique to vary the substance of their deliveries. See also *flight*.

air break A delivery that shows an appreciable movement in the air due to the bowler's skills, sometimes also helped by wind, or weather conditions.

air shot An attempted hit that fails to connect bat to ball; a shot played and missed.

all out A team is said to be all out when it loses all ten wickets. A player who is unable to bat due to injury or sickness is also considered out.

all-rounder A player who, in addition to being a competent batsman, is also a skilful bowler or wicket-keeper. Thus, the presence of an all-rounder in the team gives it greater depth or options in bowling and batting.

allotted overs The number of overs allowed for a team to bat in a one-day match. These are fixed before the commencement of the game, but may be reduced by applying an agreed formula if there is any unscheduled stoppage in play.

allow a run *(1)* Fielding side deliberately conceding a run to have the other batsman face the bowling. *(2)* Sloppy fielding that results in the batsmen taking a run which would otherwise not have been possible.

amateur Literally, a player who plays the game as a hobby and not as a profession. However, until 1962 the term referred to a classification of cricketers in England, called Amateurs (more popularly known as Gentlemen) who unlike professionals (or Players) were not entitled to receive any professional fees. Matches between amateurs and professionals were a highpoint of English county cricket until the system was abolished in 1962.

analysis See *bowling analysis*.

angle Refers to the angular direction of a delivery as it reaches the batsman, as distinct from one which is bowled in straight line with the wickets.

angled bat A gentle, straight-bat stroke, played with the face of the bat turned at an angle, rather than facing front. This helps the batsman control ball placement, while maintaining the full security of a straight-bat stroke.

angled delivery A delivery not in straight line with the pitch, but reaching the batsman somewhat diagonally. Bowlers often use the width of the bowling crease, and a slightly modified action, to bowl an angled delivery.

angling the bat A tentative and vain attempt by the batsman at playing a ball passing outside the off-stump; indicates his lack of confidence and judgement, thus giving the bowler a moral victory.

appeal A request to the umpire by the bowler or fielders to declare a batsman out, following a delivery which has resulted in a tenable case for dismissal. In reality, an appeal is more like a shout ('howzaat', or similar) than a request. According to the Laws of Cricket, an appeal must be made before a batsman can be declared out. An appeal can

appeal

also be made by the bowler or captain for change of a ball that has gone out of shape, or by a batsman against poor light.

approach *(1)* The latter part of a bowler's run-up, before delivery. *(2)* The manner in which a bowler takes his final strides before delivering the ball.

arch rivals Two teams traditionally opposed to each other, with rivalry spilling over from areas beyond the game of cricket, e.g. India and Pakistan; Oxford and Cambridge Universities.

arm A suffix describing the type of bowler (right-arm or left-arm) or the bowling style (round-arm, high-arm, etc.).

arm ball A variation delivery bowled by a finger-spinner, using the flow of arm rather than fingers to give substance to the delivery. Bowled at a slightly quicker pace than normal, an arm ball tends to drift in the opposite direction to a normal spin, thus taking the batsman by surprise. Also referred to as armer.

around the wicket See *round the wicket.*

artificial pitch A pitch which is not made of natural turf, but is laid with a synthetic material like astro-turf or cement. An artificial pitch lacks the responsiveness and variation of a natural pitch and tends to be less exciting, particularly for bowlers.

Ashes The name of the test series played between Australia and England. The term was coined after England lost a home test series to Australia for the first time in 1882. Infuriated English fans burned the stumps after the decisive test match and inserted a mock obituary in the newspapers announcing the death of English cricket and that its body would be cremated and ashes taken to Australia. Later that year when England toured Australia and won a three-test series, the fans were delighted and presented to the captain, an urn containing the real ashes of the stumps burned after the earlier series loss. The English victory was hailed by the press as 'winning the Ashes back'. The test series between England and Australia have since been called the Ashes, and the winning team is symbolically said to be in possession of the Ashes. The real Ashes are preserved at the Lord's cricket ground in London and are never moved out.

Asia cup A cricket tournament of one-day matches played every two years between the four major cricket playing nations in Asia, viz. India, Pakistan, Sri Lanka and Bangladesh. The tournament was officially begun in 1985 in Colombo.

Asian Test Championship A series of test matches played between the Asian test-playing nations to determine the best test team in Asia. The inaugural championship was played in early 1999 between India, Pakistan and Sri Lanka. Bangladesh too will now join this group, having gained test status in 2000.

asking rate *(1 one-day matches)* Runs per over required to be scored for victory by the side batting second. *(2 first-class matches)* Runs per over or per hour, required to be scored for victory by the side batting last.

associate member Refers to membership to the International Cricket Council, which is classified into full membership and associate membership. While full membership is given to test-playing countries, associate membership is granted to other countries where cricket is popular and well organised. The list of associate member countries includes Argentina, Bangladesh, Bermuda, Canada, Denmark, Fiji, Gibraltar, Hong Kong, Ireland, Israel, Kenya, Malaysia, Namibia, Papua New Guinea, the Netherlands, Singapore, the USA and the UAE.

at home *(1)* Playing at venues considered within a team's native territory, as opposed to playing in the opponent's territory or playing at neutral venues away from the base. *(2)* Said of a player or team, showing ability and confidence when performing in a given situation.

at the crease See *at the wicket*.

at the wicket *(1)* Time taken by a batsman to play an innings, e.g. 'at the wicket for two hours'. *(2)* A batsman who is not out and is continuing his innings.

attack *(1)* An aggressive approach to the game situation, whether batting, bowling, fielding or captaining. *(2)* Refers to a team's bowling attack.

attacking batsman A batsman naturally inclined to play forceful but attractive shots; one who scores runs quickly and tends to dominate the bowling.

attacking field A field setting with greater emphasis on taking catches or dismissing the batsman by putting him under pressure, than saving runs; a field setting with more fielders in catching positions and fewer in run-saving positions.

attacking interception The action of a fielder to run towards an approaching ball, pick it up and throw it in one rapid, fluid motion.

autographed bat A cricket bat signed by a famous cricketer, either as a personal memento for someone or as a commercial endorsement of its quality and workmanship.

average The mean performance of a player over a specified period. The most commonly used average measures are: 'runs per inning' for a batsman, and 'wickets per match' or 'runs per wicket' for a bowler.

away *(1)* A delivery that moves outside the off-stump, either in the air or off the pitch; considered an ideal delivery for a fast or medium fast bowler, as it increases the chances of the batsman edging a catch. *(2)* Matches played away from the team's home territory, in another city, state or country.

away-swing See *outswing*.

B b

back-cut A cut shot played to a rising ball outside the off-stump, hitting it in the arc between backward point and third man; played with the bat coming over the ball, after it has passed the batsman.

back foot The foot of the batsman that is closer to the wicket as he faces the delivery, e.g. the right foot of a right-handed batsman. Proper positioning of the back foot constitutes an important element of batting technique, particularly when playing back-foot strokes.

back-foot Refers to the strokes played by moving body and feet closer to the stumps, particularly the back foot on which much of the body weight is pivoted. Back-foot strokes allow the batsman fractionally longer to see and judge the type of delivery.

back-foot drive A basic batting stroke, played by moving quickly to the back foot and hitting the ball with a full flow of the bat. The bat is held nearly perpendicular throughout the motion, but may be slightly angled to achieve placement.

back in the pavilion Idiomatic expression for a batsman who is out.

back spin A variation delivery of a spinner, causing the ball to spin in the opposite direction, i.e., towards the bowler, rather than sideways. The ball thus loses pace, or moves differently upon pitching, surprising the batsman. It requires special skill and great control on the part of the bowler to bowl a back spin delivery effectively.

back-stop Part of the field directly behind the wicket-keeper, about halfway to the boundary line. The position exists mainly for reference and is seldom deployed during matches.

back up *(1)* One fielder covering up another to stop the ball in case the first one fails to do so. *(2)* A fielder covering up to stop a throw directed at the stumps. *(3)* The forward movement of a non-striker (batsman), along with the bowler's run-up, in preparation for a run.

backlift Initial movement of the bat from the stance position to gather momentum for a stroke. The bat goes backwards and up, in the direction of slips, before coming down on the ball.

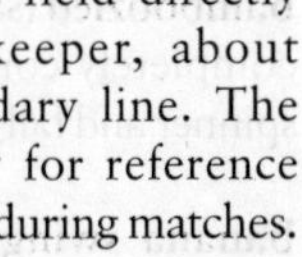

backlift

backward A part of the field or fielding position, behind an imaginary line extending from the batting crease, on either side of the wicket. The two main backward positions are *(i)* **backward square leg**, between square leg and long leg and *(ii)* **backward point**, between point and third man.

bad decision *(1)* An error of judgement by the umpire in holding the batsman out (or not out). *(2)* A strategic move on the field by a captain which proves to be an expensive error or ineffective.

bad light A situation when the light is weak enough for the umpires to consider it unsafe for batting. The batsmen are thus offered an option to stop playing until the light improves.

bad runner A batsman who does not possess the speed and judgement for good running between the wickets; one who is relatively slow and hesitant, and often gets involved in run out situations.

bad weather Persistent rain, drizzle, or similar conditions which cause the game to be stopped or delayed for a prolonged period.

bail One of the two wooden-roller pins placed on top of the stumps, each measuring 4⅜ inches in length and about 1 inch in diameter. For wicket-related dismissals (viz. bowled, stumped, hit wicket and run out), at least one bail is required to fall off for the batsman to be judged out.

bail ball A delivery that bounces to bail height and is accurate enough to dislodge the bail or nearly do so.

ball *(1)* The red cricket ball (white for day-night matches) used to play the game. A regular cricket ball measures

8¾ to 9 inches in circumference and 5½ to 5¾ ounces in weight. It is made of two hemispheres of leather stitched together with a prominent seam, and stuffed with cork and twine. A slightly smaller ball is used for women's cricket. Also known as leather. *(2)* A delivery, or type of delivery, bowled by a bowler.

ball

ball change A situation when the fielding side requests a change of ball on the grounds that the original ball in play has lost its shape.

ball-doctoring See *ball-tampering.*

ball gauge A simple, palm-sized, metallic instrument used to measure the circumference and roundness of a cricket ball. In some countries the umpires rely on this instrument to determine whether the ball has lost its shape during a match, before they allow a replacement ball to be used.

ball in play A ball is considered to be in play from the start of a bowler's run-up, until completion of the delivery and all resultant actions, like fielding, throwing, running, etc. Once all the actions are completed, the ball in play ceases and it becomes a dead ball.

balloon A misconnected shot that sends the ball straight up in the air for an easy catch. Ballooned catches come mostly off the upper part of the blade, either due to extra bounce in the delivery or the batsman's inability to play safely.

balls faced A qualitative measure of a batsman's innings. Normally, the fewer the balls faced for a given score, the more aggressive and entertaining the knock. However, situations often arise when playing for a longer time is equally important, particularly when defending the wicket to avert defeat in a first-class match.

balls to go *(1)* Countdown in terms of the number of deliveries remaining towards the end of an innings in a one-day match. *(2)* Mandatory intimation by the umpire, to a new batsman taking guard, of the number of balls remaining in the over.

ball-tampering A deliberate attempt to alter the condition of the ball to achieve extra swing, seam or turn. This may be done in a variety of ways, like picking the seam, gouging with finger nails, scrubbing on one side, etc., all of which are illegal. However, application of one's sweat to improve grip, or rubbing the ball on the trousers to improve its shine, are considered normal.

bamboozled (said of a batsman) To be completely confused by the guile of a spinner and fail to negotiate the delivery.

banana swing A freak delivery that swings excessively from the moment it leaves the bowler's hand, thus defining a banana-like trajectory. Apart from the bowler's action, newness of the ball and weather conditions can help create a banana swing. The excessive swing is, however, not necessarily effective.

bang A fast bowler's delivery, pitching the ball short of good length, with extra force generated through a pronounced body and shoulder action. The objective of such a delivery is to unsettle the batsman with lively pace and variation.

bat The wooden paddle-like implement used by a batsman to defend his wicket and play shots to score runs. It consists of a handle and a blade, joined together through a spliced cut. The maximum permitted size of a bat is 38 inches in length and 4¼ inches in breadth. Although the weight is not regulated, it normally varies between 36 and 48 ounces. All good quality bats are made of willow wood.

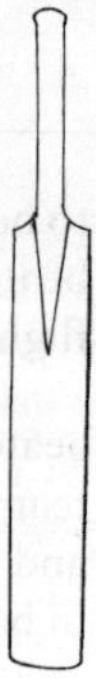
bat

bat-and-pad catch A catch coming off the edge of the bat and rebounding from the pad to be taken by a close-in fielder.

bat-and-pad gap Refers to the space between bat and pad when playing a stroke. Correct batting advocates bat and pad being close together to prevent the ball from passing through this space. Also referred to as the gate.

bat out To continue batting steadily until the completion of the innings or end of the day's play to consolidate the innings.

bat–pad position A fielding position very close to the batsman where a bat-and-pad catch is anticipated, e.g. short square leg, or silly point.

batsman *(1)* A player engaged in batting. His task is to defend his wicket and score runs, as well as to support his batting partner. *(2)* A player specialising in the art of batting and selected in the team largely on account of his ability to score runs.

batsman

batsman's paradise A ground where batting conditions are extremely favourable, i.e. an easy-paced wicket and a fast outfield.

batter A nineteenth-century term for a batsman; now used mainly in women's cricket to mean 'batswoman'.

batting The actions of a batsman to play a bowler's delivery with the bat, aiming to score runs as well as defend the wicket. It is both an individual effort, (represented by the batsman's own score), as well as a collective effort by all the batsmen in the team (total score). Proper batting requires specialised skills and is viewed as heroic as a batsman is always pitted against eleven players of the opposing team.

batting all-rounder An all-rounder whose batting skills are more prominent than his bowling skills; one who is primarily a specialist batsman and a second line bowler, e.g. Saurav Ganguly of India, or Steve Waugh of Australia.

batting average Performance measure of a batsman, indicating the mean number of runs scored per innings. It is arrived at by dividing the aggregate runs scored by the number of times dismissed. The batting average is computed separately for each stated level of cricket (tests, one-dayers, etc.) over a given period. At the highest level of cricket, a career batting average of around 35 per innings is considered good, 40 very good, 45 excellent, and 50, or above, outstanding.

batting crease (popping crease) A horizontal line drawn on the pitch, parallel to the bowling crease, at a distance of four feet in front of the wickets. The length of the batting crease is at least six feet on either side from its centre. The area behind the batting crease marks the batsman's territory.

batting line-up List of players slated to go in a particular order and bat in an innings, especially those known for their batting skills. See *batting order.*

batting order The sequence in which a team's batsmen go out to play their innings, starting with the openers (numbers 1 and 2) and ending with the last batsman at no. 11.

batting points Extra points awarded in some tournaments to the batting side for reaching a given total, within the stipulated overs. These are in addition to the points awarded for achieving an outright victory or first-innings lead, as applicable.

batting side One of the two teams in the match, taking its turn at batting. Its objective in the game is to score as many runs as it feels are necessary for victory.

batting time *(1)* Time spent by a batsman at the crease. *(2)* Time available or used by a team for batting.

beamer A fast, full-toss delivery aimed at the batsman's body. If delivered above waist height, it is called a no-ball and the umpire may also issue a warning.

beat the fielder A productive shot, with speed and placement of the ball defying a fielder's desperate attempt to stop or catch it.

beaten Failure by the batsman to play a well bowled delivery, thus missing dismissal by a close margin. The different shades of being beaten by a delivery are: **beaten all ends up** to be completely confused (by swing, pace, flight or spin) and be clueless in attempting to play a stroke; **beaten by the spin** to fail to negotiate the turn; **beaten by the swing** to misjudge the deviation in the air; **beaten by the pace** to be slow in responding to the speed; **beaten in the air** to be deceived by the flight.

beaten in all departments Said of a team suffering a comprehensive defeat and proving inferior to the opposition in batting, bowling as well as fielding.

benefit match A match played to raise funds for a nominated senior cricketer or cricket official **(beneficiary),** in recognition of his services.

benefit of doubt An appeal for dismissal ruled not out in favour of the batsman, because the umpire is not entirely satisfied that all the conditions of dismissal have been fairly met.

benefit year/season An entire cricket season of a local club or state/county team, dedicated to promote various fund-raising schemes for the beneficiary.

best bowling (or best figures) A measure of a bowler's finest achievement in the stated band of cricket.. It is measured in terms of wickets taken against runs conceded in an innings, or a match, as stated.

betting Bets may be placed in cricket on predicted match results or team/individual performances, or related events. Although officially banned in most countries, it is believed to exist unofficially at various levels and in varying degrees. A few countries, however, allow official betting, notably the United Kingdom.

big hit A powerful shot going to the boundary or a lofted shot in the deep.

big over An over in which the total jumps up considerably more than the average scoring rate, counting runs scored by the batsmen as well as extras.

bite Tendency of the ball to deviate upon pitching, largely due to the quality of the wicket, as on a damp wicket.

Black Bradman Nickname for Sir George Headley, arguably the greatest West Indian batsman. He was in his prime in the same era as Sir Don Bradman – mainly the 1930s and 1940s – but had fewer opportunities as fewer matches were played in the West Indies during that period. Nevertheless, Headley's commanding batting style, as also his numerous batting exploits in test and first-class matches, often drew comparison with Bradman and earned him the sobriquet Black Bradman. (Career record: Test matches: 2,190 runs at an average of 60.83, with 10 centuries; First-class matches: 9,921 runs at an average of 69.86, with 33 centuries.)

Black Bradman

blackwash International test cricket during the 1980s was dominated by West Indians who were considered the unofficial world champions. In 1984, when the West Indies outplayed England to register a facile 5-0 series victory, the media termed the result a 'blackwash' for England. Ever since, any 5-0 series win by the West Indies against any other country has been termed a blackwash.

blade The main portion of the bat, made of solid wood *(willow)*, which makes contact with the ball when playing strokes.

blazer The jacket of a team in the chosen colour and adorned with a crest.

blind shot Batsman taking an aimless swipe at the ball, hoping to connect somewhere and hit the ball to any part of the field. A batsman would only play this shot in desperation, to score quick runs or out of frustration when unable to cope with the bowling.

blind spot A small patch slightly outside the leg stump where the ball is momentarily unclear to the batsman as he is facing a delivery, thus forcing him to play tentatively. Leg-spinners are sometimes able to exploit this spot by getting the ball to turn around the batsman's legs for a bowled or caught behind dismissal.

blob To be out for a duck. See *duck.*

block *(1)* To play a totally defensive stroke, with little or no backlift, and keeping the body well behind the ball. *(2)* A spot near the batting crease in front of the stumps, marked by a batsman after taking guard.

block hole The position at the crease where the batsman rests his bat when facing a delivery. It is usually marked with chalk or with the toe end of the bat when taking guard.

board *(1)* Same as 'scoreboard' *(2)* The governing body for cricket affairs for the stated country, state or county.

body blow The fall of an important wicket or the loss of a key player through injury, at a critical point in the game.

body break See *action break.*

bodyline Fast, short-pitched bowling aimed at the batsman's body and employing a packed on-side attacking field. See *bodyline series.*

bodyline series The infamous test series of 1932 played between England and Australia, when the touring English side employed a strategy of attacking the Australian batsmen with fast and rising leg-side deliveries. Aimed largely at preventing Bradman from scoring heavily, the series created bitterness between the two teams because of injuries suffered by the Australian batsmen. The English attack in this series was spearheaded by the legendary fast bowler, Harold Larwood.

book cricket A game played with pen and notebook by children. Imaginary teams are selected and scores are kept by throwing dice or with a similar arrangement.

bosie An Australian colloquial term for *googly*, now obsolete.

bottom edge A misconnected shot, with ball touching the toe end or lower edge of the bat and deflecting behind the batsman.

bottom hand The lower hand gripping a bat, which provides it power and stability for playing a stroke. A shot played with a heavier bottom hand tends to have more force then finesse.

bounce The extent to which the ball rises after pitching. Depending upon the condition and type of pitch, the bounce can be high (e.g. on a fast pitch), low (slow pitch), variable (imperfect pitch) or even (normal pitch).

umpire's signal for boundary

bouncer See *bumper.*

boundary *(1)* Playing area inside the ground, marked by a peripheral line, rope or flags. On a regular cricket ground, the boundary is between 60 yards (minimum) and 90 yards (maximum) from the centre of the pitch. Four runs are scored when the ball in play (or the fielder holding it) touches the boundary. All the fielders are required to be within the boundary line before the bowler sends down a delivery. *(2)* A shot by a batsman crossing the boundary and fetching four runs; also known as *fourer.*

boundary saving A deep fielder, positioned near the boundary line with the primary objective of saving fours.

bowl *(1 bowler)* To perform a spell of bowling or send down a particular type of delivery. *(2 team)* To take the field while the opposing side bats.

bowled A common mode of dismissal wherein the batsman fails to prevent a delivery from hitting the wickets, which necessarily includes dislodging the bails. A batsman is considered bowled even if the ball deflects off his bat onto the wickets.

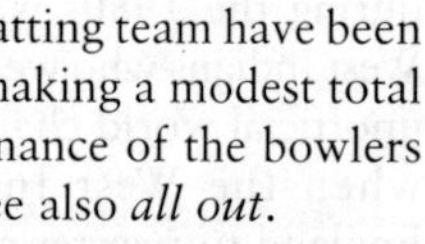
bowled

bowled out Indicates that all the batsmen of the batting team have been dismissed after making a modest total due to the dominance of the bowlers over batsmen. See also *all out*.

bowled round the legs A bowled dismissal with the delivery pitching wide outside the leg stump and taking a sharp turn to strike the wickets.

bowler *(1)* A player engaged in the act of bowling. *(2)* A player who specialises in bowling (as distinct from a batsman or wicket-keeper).

bowlers' back drive A straight drive played to the area behind the bowler. See *straight drive.*

bowlers' footmark Rough spots created near the popping crease by bowlers' boots. A delivery pitching in this area tends to turn or bounce unevenly, thus making it difficult for the batsman to negotiate.

bowlers' graveyard A pitch on which bowlers have to work hard to contain the batsmen or take wickets; a pitch that frustrates bowlers, offering no assistance for any type of bowling.

bowling *(1)* The action of sending down a delivery with the arm rolling over as the ball is released from an overhead position or a variation of it. Performed in different styles – fast, medium fast, off-spin, leg-spin, etc. – its main objective is to dismiss the batsman or contain his run scoring. *(2)* The collective performance of all the bowlers in a team during an innings, match or as a general reference.

bowling

bowling against the wind A situation in which the bowler is placed at a disadvantage due to a persistent, strong wind blowing in the direction opposite to his deliveries. This causes his bowling to lose some efficiency, through reduction in speed, difficulty in controlling the swing, etc.

bowling all-rounder An all-rounder whose bowling skills are more prominent than his batting skills; one who is normally a frontline bowler, but late order batsman. The presence of a bowling all-rounder adds depth to a team's batting, while retaining its full bowling strength, e.g. Darren Gough of England or Wasim Akram of Pakistan.

bowling analysis Refers to the statistics of the bowler's performance during an innings, match, series, etc., as stated. The standard bowling analysis is tabulated under four elements: overs, maidens, runs (conceded) and wickets. The shorter analysis shows only the last two indicators, while a more detailed one also includes economy rate and strike rate.

bowling attack A composite term for all the main bowlers in a team.

bowling average The mean bowling performance of a bowler at a given level of cricket and during a specified period (tournament, season, career, etc.). It shows the bowler's efficiency over a longer period in terms of the number of runs conceded or numbers of balls bowled, for each wicket taken.

bowling change Introduction of a new bowler to the attack, by removing one who bowled the previous over from the same end.

bowling close to the stumps A delivery bowled with the feet running closer to the stumps in order to angle it across to the batsman. The purpose of this delivery is to offer variation in an attempt to deceive the batsman.

bowling crease A straight line drawn perpendicular to the pitch, passing through the stumps. It measures four feet on either side of the stumps and marks the start of the 22-yards pitch. The bowler sends down his delivery by passing over the bowling crease, but without crossing the popping crease drawn four feet ahead.

bowling machine A mechanical device that ejects the ball with pace, swing or spin identical to real bowling. It is used for batting practice, but is rarely available or used outside Australia and England.

bowling mark The spot from which a bowler commences his bowling run-up; usually marked by placing a visible object or by scrubbing a line with the foot.

bowling partner The longer term operation of two bowlers, bowling in tandem, and forming a formidable partnership; each bowler is a partner to the other, complimenting as well as competing against the other in wicket taking, e.g. Lilly and Thompson (Australia), Bedi and Prasanna (India).

bowling points Extra points awarded to a team in some tournaments for taking a specified number of wickets during an innings. These are in addition to the points awarded for achieving an outright victory or first-innings lead, as applicable.

bowling side One of the two teams in a match, taking its turn to bowl and dismiss the opponents (the batting side). Its objective in the game is to restrict the batting side to a small total so as to achieve a victory. Also referred to as the fielding side.

bowling to the field Accurate bowling forcing the batsman to play shots to the set field, thus restricting run scoring.

bowling wide of the crease A delivery bowled from the edge of the crease, away from the stumps, so that the ball reaches the batsman at an acute angle. It is bowled as a variation to the normal delivery in an attempt to deceive the batsman.

bowling with the wind A situation in which the wind blows from behind the bowler, thus affording him some assistance by way of improved speed, swing or drift in the delivery.

box See *abdominal guard.*

brace Two runs scored from a single delivery, with both the batsmen crossing over twice from one side to the other.

Bradman Sir Donald Bradman, the greatest batsman the game has ever produced. Playing for Australia between 1928 and 1948, Bradman amassed 6,996 runs in only 52 tests at an incredible average of 99.94 runs per innings. He scored 29 test centuries, including three triple centuries and ten double centuries. His exploits in first-class cricket were equally impressive, scoring 28,067 runs with 117 centuries at an average of over 95.14 per innings. Great batting accomplishments are often compared with Bradman, or referred to as being Bradmanesque.

Bradman

Bradman era The period of the 1930s and 1940s, famous for Bradman's awesome batting exploits. This period was noted for opposition teams trying various strategies to contain Bradman and aiming for higher totals to avoid defeat.

break *(1)* A delivery that turns, or deviates after pitching; an off-break or a leg-break. *(2)* A scheduled stoppage in play, e.g. lunch break.

break the partnership Dismissal of one of the two batsmen who are associated, or are threatening to be associated, in a long partnership.

break-through The timely taking of the wicket of a prized batsman or a much-awaited dismissal after a long partnership.

bucket hands Said of a fielder reputed for safe catching, particularly in slips and close-in positions; a fielder who unfailingly takes sharp catches with natural ease and anticipation.

buffet ball A very easy delivery which the batsman effortlessly dispatches to the boundary.

building up an innings Systematic approach by a batsman to play a long innings, taking the time to settle in, before progressively broadening the strokeplay and accelerating run scoring.

bumped catch An invalid catch, with bat, ball and ground coming into contact at the same time. It may also refer to an invalid catch when the ball touches the ground just before being taken by a fielder.

bumper A fast, short-pitched delivery that bounces high, reaching the batsman at shoulder height or above. Used as a weapon by fast bowlers to surprise or intimidate batsmen, it requires a great deal of extra pace and precision to be effective. Also referred to as *bouncer*.

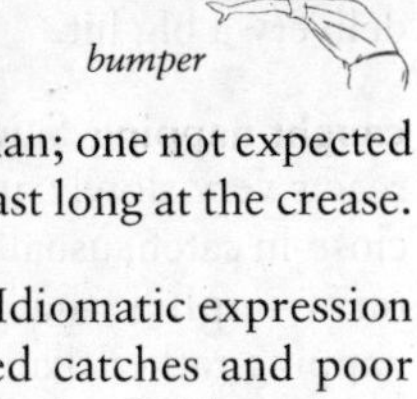

bumper

bunny with the bat A poor batsman; one not expected to score runs or last long at the crease.

butterfingers *(1)* Idiomatic expression to describe spilled catches and poor fielding. *(2)* Said of a fielder who is unable to hold catches.

buy a wicket To dismiss a batsman with a catch or by stumping, after allowing him to pick easy runs off seemingly similar deliveries just before. Also refers to a bowling tactic to entice a batsman into playing bold strokes which eventually lead to his dismissal.

bye Runs scored from a missed shot, after the ball crosses the stumps and the wicket-keeper too fails to stop it or fails to prevent the batsmen from crossing over. Such runs are added to the total of extras.

umpire's signal for bye

C c

call A loud shout by one of the two batsmen at the crease to start for a run or stay at the crease.

Calypso Nickname for the West Indian style of cricket; originally the word refers to traditional Caribbean songs and music.

cap *(1)* A close fitting, soft, peak cap, often made distinctive by the team colour and monogram. *(2)* The tradition of presenting a team cap to a new player when he plays his first match, indicating selection to a higher team or the achievement of a notable performance.

capped A new player included in the team.

captain The player appointed as a leader of the team; one responsible for marshalling the team's resources and implementing the strategy to achieve a victory.

captain to captain An expression describing the relatively uncommon situation of a captain bowling to the opposing captain during an innings, thus creating an interesting contest within a contest.

captain's knock A responsible batting display by the captain, scoring a notable number of runs, as well as holding the innings together to help register a decent total.

career best A player's all time best performance during an innings or match, as stated; e.g. the highest individual score of a batsman, the best bowling performance of a bowler, or the highest number of dismissals by a wicket-keeper.

Caribbean Of, or relating to, the West Indies, which includes many independent island countries in the Caribbean sea. The Caribbean has produced some of the finest cricketers including George Headley, Gary Sobers, Clive Lloyd, Rohan Kanhai, Brian Lara and Viv Richards.

carpet Refers to the playing field when covered with thick grass.

carry An uppish or thin-edged stroke that travels in the air up to a fielder on its own momentum.

carry the bat Said of an opening batsman who bats right through the innings and remains not out at the fall of the last wicket.

cart track An extremely cracked wicket – one resembling a cart track – on which the ball turns and bounces unpredictably, thus making batting very difficult.

castle Stumps are sometimes referred to as a castle. The batsman defends his stumps much as a soldier defended a castle.

catch

catch To hold a ball going up in the air, before it lands on the ground. A catch coming off the bat results in the loss of a wicket, providing the delivery is not a no-ball and the catch is taken inside the boundary line.

catches win matches A famous cricketing maxim, stressing the importance of taking catches.

catching machine A specially-fabricated, metal or wooden table, used for catching practice. It has a curved or slanted surface and the practice ball thrown on it bounces and deviates off the top, thus testing the fielder's agility. Also called *cradle*.

catching position A field placement primarily intended for taking catches closer to the batsman, like slips, gully, short square leg, etc.

caught A catch taken to dismiss a batsman. It is the most common mode of dismissal, abbreviated in the scorecard as 'c'.

caught and bowled A dismissal (of the batsman) by a catch which is taken by the bowler himself.

caught behind A dismissal (of the batsman) by a catch taken by the wicket-keeper behind the stumps.

caught in the deep A catch taken by a fielder near the boundary line, indicating that the batsman attempted to give the delivery a big hit.

caught napping Said of a fielder who reacts very slowly and floors a simple close-in catch, usually in the slips. The term implies that the fielder was napping rather than being alert.

caught on the wrong foot Said of a batsman who falters in his footwork when playing a stroke and ends up clumsily beaten, bowled or lbw.

Ceat rankings International cricket ranking for national teams as well as individual players, based upon the current year's performances. Sponsored by Ceat, a multinational company, the ranking is based on a system of points and updated results are periodically published by the media.

cement wicket An artificial pitch made of concrete. It is used in some countries for club or divisional-level matches where a regular turf, or matting wicket is not available. A cement wicket, however, lacks the responsiveness of a turf wicket and is never used for first-class matches.

centurion A batsman who scores a century.

century A score of one hundred or more runs by an individual batsman; a notable achievement at any level of cricket, more so at the higher levels.

century before lunch The exceptional achievement by a batsman of scoring one hundred or more runs before lunch in a test or first-class match. So far only four batsmen have achieved this feat in test matches. They are Victor Trumper, Charles Mcartney, Don Bradman (all from Australia) and Majid Khan (Pakistan).

century in each innings The rare achievement by a batsman of scoring one hundred or more runs in each of the two innings of a test or first-class match.

century of centuries The hundredth first-class century of a batsman's career, including test centuries. To date, only 24 batsmen have achieved this very exceptional batting feat.

century on debut The distinction of a batsman scoring one hundred, or more, runs in his very first match at the stated level of cricket, e.g. test, first-class or one-day matches.

challenging target A total required for victory that is neither easy nor out of reach; a target requiring considerable skill and application by the batting side to attain it.

chance A missed opportunity to dismiss a batsman due to a dropped catch, a fumbled stumping or failure to run out.

chanceless A notable knock by a batsman or a substantial partnership between two batsmen, without offering any chance to be dismissed.

change bowler A bowler not considered one of the main bowlers in the side, but brought in to bowl a short spell to give the batsmen some new bowling to face or offer relief to the regular bowlers.

change end *(1)* A bowler taken out of attack from one side and brought in to bowl immediately from the opposite side. *(2)* A batsman taking one run (or three runs) on the last ball of the over to go to the opposite end to face a fresh over.

change of pace A variation delivery bowled at a deceptively slower pace than normal in an attempt to deceive the batsman and cause him to mistime the stroke; more effectively bowled by fast bowlers or medium pacers.

change of shape Said of a cricket ball which loses shape prematurely due to factors like poor quality, hard ground, rough batting surface or excessive hammering by the batsmen. A ball that goes out of shape during an innings is allowed to be replaced by a similar, used ball.

charge Aggressive intent on the part of a player, particularly a batsman stepping out of his crease to play an attacking shot.

charmed innings/life A lucky knock by a batsman, escaping dismissal on account of missed chances or close calls going in his favour.

chase *(1)* A team in pursuit of the targeted runs for victory, batting second in a one-day match or batting last in a first-class match. *(2)* A batsman playing, or attempting to play an unwarranted stroke to a delivery going harmlessly outside the off-stump.

cherry A cricket ball is sometimes referred to as a cherry, because of its colour (red) and its resemblance to the fruit.

chest pad Protective padding worn by a batsman to avoid chest injuries from the rising deliveries of fast bowlers. Introduced during the 1932 bodyline series, it has not proved very popular and batsmen avoid using it as much as possible.

chin strap A thin padded strap, attached to the batsman's helmet, worn on the chin for protection against rising deliveries.

Chinaman A wrist-spin delivery bowled by a slow left-arm spinner, which turns like an off-break for a right-hand batsman. In some countries, the term is used to describe a left-arm wrist spinner's delivery that turns the other way, i.e. a left-arm googly.

Chinese cut An inner-edge cut, deflecting the ball in the opposite direction to that intended, mostly behind the wicket-keeper or to fine leg. The stroke is often entertaining to watch as the batsman does not know exactly where the ball has gone.

chip shot A lofted shot placed over the head of the fielders to land in a vacant area.

chop A kind of a cut shot, played to a ball outside the off-stump, with the bat coming over the ball to hit it into the ground. Although lacking in power, the chop is a very safe shot to execute and is used to place the ball in the backward point or third man region.

chuck An unfair bowling action in which the bowler straightens his bowling arm just before delivery. A bowler who bowls with such an action is called a chucker and the delivery is declared a no-ball if spotted by the umpire.

circle The oval-shaped marking around the pitch to regulate play in one-day matches. It is formed by connecting two semicircles of 30 yards radius each, drawn from the stumps at either end. (The term 'circle' is, thus, a misnomer.) Fielding sides are restricted from placing more than two fielders outside the circle during the first 15 overs of an innings. The intent of this rule is to discourage fielding sides from playing a purely defensive game from the start.

classical batsman An elegant batsman, always displaying copybook technique and playing a wide range of strokes.

clean bowled A bowled dismissal, emphasising that the delivery comprehensively struck the

clean bowled

stumps, rather than just dislodged the bails.

clear day An ideal day for playing cricket, with adequate sunlight, few clouds and no disturbing winds.

clear hit A well connected, lofted shot placed away from the fielders, and often good enough to fetch a boundary.

clearing the ropes To hit a lofted shot for six runs; to send the ball sailing over the boundary.

climb The prolonged and disconcerting bounce of a fast bowler's delivery, generally after pitching short of good length.

clip A neat deflection off the legs to the area around square leg and mid-wicket. The shot relies on good timing and wrist work, rather than power, and is effectively used against pace bowlers to pick runs in singles or twos.

clobber Relentless attack on the bowling, with powerful hits.

close call A risky run which could have resulted in the batsman being run out.

close catching position Fielding positions which are only a few yards away from the batsman, e.g. short square leg or silly point.

close finish A tantalising final session of a match which ends in victory with a very narrow margin for a team, after going through a period of uncertainty when either a defeat or draw/tie also appeared possible.

close-in catch A catch taken within a couple of yards from the batsman, at any of the close catching positions, such as silly mid-off, silly mid-on, short square leg, etc.

close-in fielder A fielder placed at any of the close catching positions. The term also applies to a specialist fielder, reputed for taking sharp catches close to the wicket.

close of play End of the day's play at the stipulated time for test and first-class matches. In one-day matches, 'close of play' signifies the end of the match itself. See also *draw of stumps.*

close the face To play a safe, defensive shot, turning the bat inwards and making sure the ball does not go off the edge and carry to slips or other close-in fielders.

cloudy skies Indicating dull and murky weather conditions not ideal for a game of cricket. Such conditions prove difficult for batting, but can be helpful for pace or swing bowling.

club cricket Matches played between local or inter-state clubs which are below the rank of first-class cricket recognition.

coach A person appointed to train the players of a team, being an experienced former cricketer himself, or one with technical qualifications in cricket coaching.

code of conduct Established traditions of the game, not covered by the Laws of Cricket, but expected to be followed by the players, e.g. not questioning the umpire's decision.

coffin An extra long and roomy, soft bag used by the players to carry their personal cricketing equipment, like bats, pads, gloves, etc.

collar (collar the bowling) To score runs at a brisk pace, thrashing the bowling to all parts of the ground.

collision One player inadvertently bumping into another during the course of play; e.g., a batsman colliding with a fielder.

coloured clothing Refers to the non-traditional, coloured cricketing attire used in some one-day matches, particularly those with large commercial sponsorships. Such clothing is, however, mandatory in day-night matches.

coming in *(1)* A fast bowler's delivery angling, seaming, or swinging towards the batsman from off, or outside the off-stump. *(2)* New batsman coming to bat at the fall of a wicket.

competitive score A moderate total put up by the team batting first, which gives its bowlers a fair chance to defend, or bowl the opposition out.

compile To bat in a careful and purposeful manner, aiming to reach a pre-determined individual, or team score.

comprehensively beaten Said of a batsman who is confused by a delivery and misses playing it by a wide margin.

contract player An external player engaged by a club or state/country board to play matches for a stipulated period, in return for a financial consideration.

copybook style Orthodox style, conforming to the coaching books. The term is more applicable to batting due to the wider scope for technicalities involved in playing different strokes.

cordon An attacking field arrangement, with a cluster of fielders placed in an arc around the batsman. It includes some or all of the following positions: gully, up to four slips, leg slip and short fine leg, besides the wicket-keeper.

corridor (corridor of uncertainty) A narrow, imaginary band along the good length area, in line between off-stump and just outside. Batsmen are often vulnerable to deliveries pitched in this area due to uncertainty regarding the kind of stroke to be played.

counter attack Instance of a batsman going for shots when confronted with hostile bowling or an attacking field setting.

county cricket The premier English domestic cricket championship, played between April and September each year. Begun in 1890, it currently involves 18 first-class county teams, playing four-day matches on a league basis. The team securing the maximum points tally is awarded the **county championship** title for the year.

cover drive A drive played to a ball pitching on or outside the off-stump, dispatching it to the covers region. A graceful and flowing stroke, it can be played off the front, or back foot. If well executed, it shows the batsman's authority and style, particularly if the ball is placed well enough to beat the fielders.

cover point A fielding position on the off-side, between extra cover and point. A fielder in that position. Its (or the fielder's) main purpose is to stop a batsman from taking short singles by pushing the ball in the cover or point areas. Captains often prefer to place their most agile fielder in this position.

cover shot Any shot played in the covers region, e.g. drive or cut.

cover up The action of a fielder to position himself behind another fielder as a backup in case the latter misfields. This is basic fielding discipline followed in situations when a sharp return is sent to the bowler or wicket-keeper who may not be able to collect it properly.

covers *(1)* A large fielding area on the off-side, between point and mid-off, comprising all the three cover positions—extra cover, cover and cover point. *(2)* Also refers to the covers that are used to protect the pitch from rainwater or moisture.

cowshot A powerful, cross-batted shot, played with the batsman going down on one knee and picking an outside the off-stump delivery on half-volley to hit it anywhere between deep mid-wicket and deep mid-on. Unorthodox and risky, it can be very productive and is exciting to watch if well executed.

cracked wicket A dry and crumbled wicket on which the ball turns and bounces unpredictably. The wicket thus proves extremely difficult for batting, while helping spin and medium pace bowlers who are also able to get extra turn and cut off the pitch.

cradle See *catching machine.*

cramped for room A batsman unable to play the intended shot, due to misjudgement of the delivery or unexpected deviation after pitching, leaving him in an imperfect position to execute the shot.

crease Lines drawn at both the ends of the pitch to regulate batting, bowling and running between the wickets. These comprise: *(i)* bowling crease, *(ii)* batting or popping crease and *(iii)* return crease.

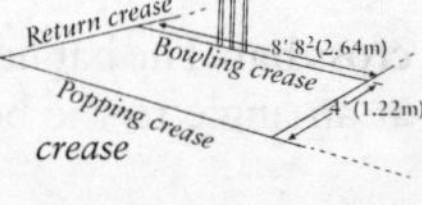

CricInfo A popular website providing extensive, worldwide cricket news and information through the Internet. In particular, it provides the latest scores of all tests and one-day international matches, as well as updated cricketing statistics for a number of players. Two of the other sites are khel.com and clickcricket.com.

cricket An outdoor game, played with bat and ball, between two teams of eleven players each. The teams take turns at batting and bowling and abide by the Laws of Cricket. The objective of the game is to register a victory by scoring more runs than the opponents. Matches are played for varying lengths of time, starting from as low as half-a-day at club level, going up to five days for a test match. The game is governed by official boards appointed for each state/country and is administered at the highest level by the International Cricket Council, headquartered in London. The origins of the game are traced back to fourteenth-century England. However, the game was only really established during the seventeenth century and has since seen many changes in rules, equipment, attire, etc.

cricket bag A specially made, long bag for carrying the many items comprising a player's personal cricket gear, like bats, pads, gloves, balls, trousers, shoes, etc. Also known as holdall.

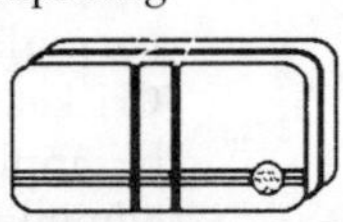
cricket bag

cricket gear The complete personal equipment of a cricket player. Apart from several sets of clothing and caps, a complete set of cricket gear includes boots and socks, bats and balls, pads and gloves, box and arm guards, and several sundry items like bat grips, bat tape, inner gloves, sweat bands, etc.

cricket ground A cricket ground is distinguished by the 22-yard pitch in the centre. The ideal ground is oval shaped, marked by a boundary line at a radius of between 60 to 75 yards from the pitch. The other common features of a cricket ground, though not essential for junior cricket, are a pavilion, a scoreboard and two sight-screens.

cricket kit A large and sturdy canvas bag to carry the team's playing equipment, which includes several bats, pads, stumps, gloves and balls.

cricket memorabilia Sundry cricketing artefacts (photographs, trophies, bats, caps, stumps, etc.) belonging to renowned cricketing personalities or associated with memorable cricketing events. Many of the well established cricket grounds sport a collection of cricket memorabilia, the most famous one being at the Lord's cricket ground in London.

cricket quiz An indoor game, or activity, testing the knowledge of the participants about cricketing events and personalities, as well as its abounding records and statistics.

cricket rules The game of cricket is played by the Laws of Cricket, formulated by the International Cricket Council. Additional rules may be applied locally for purposes of administration (e.g. qualification of players, number of overs in a limited-overs match, etc.) and may be separately laid down for each tournament.

cricketer A person who plays cricket regularly for a recognised club or team.

cricketer of the year An award given to a cricketer for his impressive performances during the year or over a number of years. The award is presented by an organisation or the governing board of cricket for the region/country and is normally presented at the end of the cricketing season. Several such awards may exist in different countries/regions, and there could also be several cricketers presented with this award each year. In India, five cricketers are chosen every year by the publishers of *Indian Cricket* for the 'Cricketer of the Year' award.

cricketeress A woman cricketer. The term is not normally used today, the more common term being cricketer.

Cricketers Benefit Fund Series A biannual international cricket tournament played in Sharjah, UAE. For each tournament, 3 or 4 national teams are invited to participate and cash awards are presented based on results. Benefit purses are also presented after each tournament to the nominated cricketers.

cricketers' injuries Bruises and blows are all part of the game of cricket and considered casual injuries. The more serious cricketing injuries affect the shoulder, back and knees, particularly in the latter part of a cricketer's career. Fast bowlers are more prone to these injuries than batsmen or spinners.

cross The moment, or position during a run when the two batsmen at the wicket cross each other to get to the opposite ends.

cross bat The bat held horizontally or at an angle to the body, such as for a pull, hook, cut or sweep. Although generating considerable power, cross-batted strokes are risky because the chances of connecting bat to ball are lower than with straight-bat strokes. Such strokes are, therefore, not recommended when the batsman is unsure of which way the delivery will bounce and deviate after pitching.

crowd invasion Hold up in play due to a large number of spectators running onto the field. Although much controlled today, this still occurs when the spectators intend congratulating a player for an achievement or protest against the home team's poor performance. See also *pitch invasion.*

crowding the batsman The placement of many fielders around the batsman in anticipation of a close catch or simply to put pressure on the batsman.

crumble A weak batting performance, resulting in the team being dismissed for a poor total.

crumbling wicket A pitch that starts disintegrating due to hot and dry weather, or wear and tear, particularly towards the latter part of a match. Consequently, the ball bounces unpredictably after pitching and helps bowlers (especially spinners and medium pacers), at the expense of batsmen.

curator A person responsible for preparing and monitoring a turf wicket; known in some countries as a groundsman.

curing The prolonged preparation of a cricket wicket through watering, mowing, rolling and technical supervision.

curl A spinner's delivery with a pronounced arc-like movement and deviation of the ball in the air or an appreciable turn off the wicket.

cut A shot played with a horizontal bat or as near horizontal as possible, hitting the ball to cover, point or third man areas. It is a forceful shot, typically played off the back foot to balls coming up after pitching. See also *late cut, back-cut* and *forward-cut.*

cutter *(1)* A medium paced delivery that deviates after pitching due to the bowler's action. See also *off-cutter, leg-cutter. (2)* A batsman who uses the cut shots frequently and to good effect.

D d

dab A defensive shot, played tentatively to a ball outside the off-stump; often the result of late judgement, leaving little time for the batsman to play a more forceful shot.

damp pitch Pitch affected by rain, or moisture seeping through the covers, thus playing unpredictably and making batting very difficult.

dancing down the wicket A stroke played by the batsman stepping out of his crease and hitting the ball firmly, at full or half-volley, in front of the wickets. The stroke is executed with graceful footwork and precision timing, making it stylish and enjoyable to watch.

dancing down the wicket

danger area Refers to the area of the pitch, in front of the batsman, on which the bowlers' deliveries land. All players, particularly batsmen and bowlers, are prevented from running on this area in order to protect it from possible damage.

danger end *(1)* The side of the wickets where the main action is directed to dismiss a batsman. *(2)* The side to which a fielder throws the ball in an attempt to run out the batsman.

day–night match A limited-overs match which commences in the afternoon and carries on until completion in the night, with the latter half played under floodlights.

umpire's signal for dead ball

dead ball A ball is said to be dead when all actions of play connected with it are completed—i.e. delivery bowled, ball fielded, run(s) scored, wicket taken, etc. There is always a brief period when the ball is dead between one delivery and the next.

dead bat

dead bat A totally defensive stroke played with little backlift, or follow-through. The bat is also angled down, so that the ball comes to a stop within a few yards from the batsman.

dead wicket/pitch A slow and lifeless pitch which neither offers any assistance to the bowlers, nor is conducive to strokeplay. It is characterised by a slow scoring rate and fewer wickets falling, and is generally unexciting, as compared with a normal pitch.

death rattle The sound which a batsman hears when he misses a delivery and is comprehensively bowled, thus marking the end of his innings.

debut The first match of a player's career in the stated division of cricket, e.g. test, first-class, one-dayers, etc.

deck Refers to the pitch, particularly when it is hard and bouncy. The term is not commonly used.

declare (declaration) To close the innings before all ten wickets have fallen. This is done by the captain of the batting team when he believes his team has scored enough runs for his bowlers to have a go at the opposing team.

declared out A batsman given out by the umpire under doubtful or debatable circumstances.

deep *(1)* A prefix applied to a field position, indicating a relatively longer distance from the batsman, e.g. deep cover, deep mid-off, etc. *(2)* Part of the outfield which is nearer the boundary.

deep batting line-up A team strong in batting; one having several all-rounders and a wicket-keeper capable of scoring runs, in addition to the regular batsmen.

deep field A collective term for the positioning of fielders closer to the boundary line. A deep field is set mainly to control run scoring, and indicates dominance of batting or defensive play by the fielding side.

deep fielder A fielder positioned in the outfield, i.e. at a distance from the batsman, nearer the boundary line.

defence The batting skill used to play defensively, with the main aim of protecting the wicket rather than scoring runs.

defence

defend To bat with the aim of protecting the wicket, rather than to score runs.

defend the total Said of a situation when the bowling side tries to restrict the opposition from overtaking its total score.

defensive field A field setting that places greater emphasis on saving runs than on taking catches or putting the batsman under pressure; one with a majority of the fielders in the outfield and very few in close-in positions.

deficit The number of runs by which a team's total is short of the opponent's total at any stage of the game.

deflect A leg-side stroke played gently by turning the bat at the precise moment of impact with the ball, placing it over a wide area between square leg and fine leg. The bat is held nearly perpendicular when executing the stroke, making it very safe. It is most effective against pace bowlers, as the natural bounce and speed of the delivery can be used to good effect.

delay *(1)* A game unable to commence, or resume due to an external factor like rain, unfit ground conditions, crowd disturbance, etc. *(2)* Temporary hold-up in play due to an internal factor like injury to a player, change of ball, awaiting the third umpire's decision, etc.

delaying tactics Deliberate slowing down of the game by a team to leave the opposition with less time to press for a win. A negative and unsporting ploy, it may be resorted to in test or first-class matches, but has no relevance in one-day matches.

deliberate padding A conscious attempt by a batsman to block or deflect a delivery with his pad, rather than his bat. This is done when the batsman avoids playing a delivery that can result in a close-in catch. Deliberate padding can, however, cause a dismissal by lbw if the other conditions are met.

deliver To send down a ball with proper bowling action.

delivery *(1)* A ball sent down by a bowler. *(2)* The basic unit of bowling, with six valid deliveries comprising an over. *(3)* The bowling action of a bowler.

depth The extra capabilities a team has in the batting and/or bowling departments, over and above the usual number of specialists. This is often the result of having good all-rounders on the side.

dew Refers to morning dew on a pitch, especially in cool weather conditions. Its presence helps fast bowlers get an extra nip or seam off the wicket. Thus, special note is taken of the presence of dew when assessing the wicket condition at the start of a day's play.

did not bat A notation on a scoresheet or a player's personal record book, indicating no opportunity to bat in the innings. This can happen in a number of situations, like declaration of the innings, the team achieving the victory target, unscheduled stoppage in play, etc. For statistical purposes, 'did not bat' is not counted as an innings played, although it is counted as a match played.

difficult decision An appeal for dismissal where both 'out' and 'not out' possibilities exist and the umpire has to deliberate a while before giving his decision.

dig in A delivery bowled with extra pace and pronounced body action to get the ball to bounce up after pitching.

dig out Said of a batsman who manages to offer the bat to a yorker just in time to prevent the ball from passing underneath the bat. See *yorker.*

dip A flighted delivery that loses height abruptly and pitches a shade shorter than anticipated. The ability to dip the delivery often distinguishes a good spinner from an ordinary one.

direct hit A quick return by a fielder that hits the wickets. It can be dramatic when the batsman is run out or narrowly escapes dismissal.

direct throw A return from a deep fielder, sending the ball sharply and accurately to the bowler or wicket-keeper.

direction The line of a delivery in relation to the stumps, viz. on stumps, outside off-stump or outside leg stump. Along with length, direction is one of the basic attributes of effective bowling.

dismissal The fall of a batsman's wicket or the manner in which a batsman's innings is brought to an end, e.g. bowled, run out, lbw, etc.

dismissed *(1 batsman)* To lose the wicket or get out. *(2 bowler)* To capture a wicket. *(3 team)* To be all out or to bowl out the opposition.

dissent The action, or body language of a player indicating disagreement with the umpire's decision. In tests and one-day internationals, a player showing dissent is liable to be penalised by the referee of the match.

dive The action of a player in throwing himself onto the ground in a desperate attempt to take a catch, field a ball or complete a run.

diving catch Catch falling slightly out of reach of a fielder, but held inches off the ground by lunging forward or sideways and falling in the process.

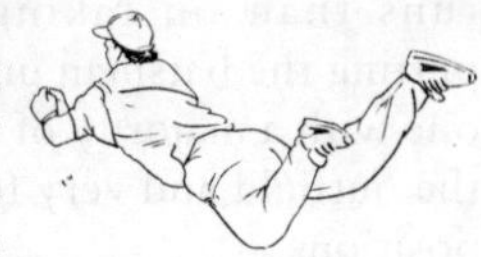

diving catch

dolly/dolly catch A very simple and straight forward catch. *See lolly.*

dominant role Said of a batsman who plays a dominant role and scores the bulk of the total runs scored in a partnership or an innings.

donkey drop A high flight delivery pitched short of length, giving the batsman an easy opportunity to take a powerful hit. A donkey drop is seldom bowled on purpose and is generally the result of an error by the bowler.

doosra A vernacular (Urdu/Hindi) term coined by the Pakistani cricket team to distinguish the special delivery of their famous off-spinner, Saqlain Mushtaq. The delivery is bowled with a regular off-spin action but deviates in the opposite direction (i.e. leg to off) upon pitching, thus deceiving the batsman. The term means 'the other one', and became famous in 1999 after Saqlain's remarkable success in troubling batsmen (while taking several wickets) by the frequent use of this delivery.

dot ball An uneventful delivery with no runs scored or wicket taken. Such a delivery is recorded in the scoresheet with a dot.

double An impressive performance registered by a player in batting as well as bowling (or batting and wicket-keeping), during a match, series, season or career. Runs scored for a double are usually ten times the number of wickets (dismissals) taken, in rounded numbers. Thus, in English county cricket, scoring 1000 runs and taking 100 wickets in a season is a notable double.

double blow The occurrence in quick succession of two unfavourable events for a team, e.g. the quick fall of two wickets when batting or the non-availability of two bowlers due to injury.

double century (double hundred) Score of two hundred or more runs by a batsman in a single innings. It is a significant batting landmark for tests and first-class matches and has not yet been achieved in the limited-over games.

double change A situation when the captain brings in new bowlers to bowl at both ends of the wicket in successive overs.

double spin attack Operation of spin bowlers from both ends of the wicket, particularly when bowling to an attacking field.

double wicket cricket A non-official form of cricket, played to determine the best pair of cricketers in the group invited to participate. Certain ad hoc rules are applied when playing such games, which are mainly held for the purpose of exhibition.

doubtful decision An appeal for dismissal upheld by the umpire, but leaving other observers unconvinced of the validity of the decision.

dour batsman A batsman who is naturally inclined to bat in a safe and controlled manner, relying mainly on quiet placements or bad deliveries to score runs and avoiding any risky shots.

dour batting/knock Slow and unexciting batting, although scoring valuable runs. Mainly seen in test or first-class cricket, but unusual for one-day matches.

down *(1)* A part of the team score, indicating the number of wickets lost by the batting side, e.g. four down for 100 runs. *(2)* Any batting position after the openers, as indicated by the number of wickets fallen, e.g. six down, meaning to bat after the fall of the sixth wicket.

drag A cross-batted shot, resembling an elaborate pull, hitting the ball from outside the off-stump to mid-on or mid-wicket area.

drag the ball A misconnected pull, or cut that results in the ball rolling onto the stumps.

draw An incomplete match in which neither side wins, i.e. the result is neither win/lose, nor a tie.

draw away A batsman's action in moving body and feet towards the leg-side to make extra room to play the ball on the off-side. An unorthodox manner of batting, it is mainly resorted to when attempting to score quick runs, or to upset the bowling and field setting.

draw of stumps End of the day's play for a match scheduled over more than one day.

draw out To bowl a well-pitched delivery that forces the batsman to stretch forward or come out of the crease to play a stroke. The term applies mainly to spinners bowling well-flighted and enticing deliveries.

dressing room A special room reserved in the pavilion for players to rest and get ready in, as well as to keep their personal bags and belongings.

drifter A spinner's flighted delivery that deviates in the air, making it difficult for the batsman to pick its line. It is mainly bowled as a variation delivery to deceive the batsman.

drinks break A five minute suspension of play within a session for the players to have a drink and rest.

drinks cart A large, wheeled trolley, or small cart on which drinks are carried to the field during the drinks break. For high profile matches, the drinks cart may be painted with the logo and colours of the match sponsor, if any.

drive A basic batting stroke in which the ball is hit firmly with a straight flow of the bat. Depending upon the line and length of the delivery, it can be played in a variety of ways: off the front foot, off the back foot or on the rise. Depending upon the skill of the batsman, the drive can be placed in a wide arc in front of the wickets, from point to mid-wicket.

drop *(1 fielding)* To fail to hold on to a possible catch. *(2 batting)* The position at which a batsman goes in to bat, after a wicket has fallen, e.g. one drop, two drop. *(3 player)* To be left out of the team or not be selected.

drop short *(1 fielding)* A catch that falls in front of or just out of reach of the fielder. *(2 bowling)* A delivery pitched short of good length.

dropped *(1)* A missed catch. *(2)* A batsman offered a lease of life due to a missed catch. *(3)* A player left out or not selected in the team.

dropping ball The descent of the ball after it is hit high and attains the maximum height of the particular trajectory.

dry pitch A pitch devoid of any life and moisture, hence discouraging for bowlers, particularly fast bowlers.

duck *(1)* Short for 'duck's egg', meaning a batsman dismissed for zero. **Duck out** thus means to be dismissed without scoring. *(2 batting)* To move the head away quickly or to suddenly lower the body to let the ball pass over particularly when avoiding a bouncer.

duck

Duckworth–Lewis formula An official rain-rule formula used in the World Cup and other one-day international matches to compute the revised number of overs when the playing time is cut short by rain, or bad weather. The formula is named after its two UK-based inventors, Frank Duckworth (a consultant/statistician) and Tony Lewis (a lecturer in mathematics).

E e

ear cover A hard, circular flap attached to a batsman's helmet to protect the ear against injury that may be caused by a rising delivery.

early blow The batting side losing one or two important wickets at the start of an innings or on resumption of play.

early swing A pace bowler's delivery that starts deviating in the air immediately after leaving the bowler's hand. The early swing is, however, not necessarily effective as the ball tends to go off target and the batsman also gets a fraction longer to judge its movement.

earn a cap *(1)* A new player who makes a debut for a higher grade team. *(2)* A player inducted into the senior team in recognition of his talents.

eastern gallery Spectators' stand on the eastern side of the ground, normally reserved for tickets less expensively priced as it faces the afternoon sun.

easy chance An easy opportunity for dismissal squandered by a mistake on the part of the fielders, like a catch dropped or run out missed.

economical A bowler who does not concede many runs or a bowling spell in which runs are difficult to score.

economy rate The average performance of a bowler in terms of runs conceded per over or runs conceded per hundred balls; applies to the stated level of cricket, as well as to the stated period (match, season, career, etc.).

edge *(1)* The sharp, long corners of the bat, comprising the **outer edge** (away from the batsman) and the **inner edge** (closer to the batsman). *(2)* Ball deflecting behind the stumps from the corner of the bat. It is further classified as a **thin edge** (ball touching the bat lightly) or a **thick edge** (ball touching the bat firmly).

elbow pad Protective strip of padding worn by a batsman on the upper hand holding the bat to avoid injury from a rising delivery.

eleven (XI) A team comprising players selected from an ad hoc grouping, as opposed to a recognised club, state or county team, e.g. Board President's XI, Universities XI, etc.

end *(1)* Either of the two sides of the pitch from which batting and bowling is performed—referred to as **batting end** and **bowling end** or **striker's end** and **non-striker's end**, respectively. *(2)* A suffix referring to the direction of the ground, e.g. pavilion end or far end.

English summer The summer in England, starting early April and going up to late September, during which cricket is played intensively at all levels. The high point of the English summer is the test and one-day series between England and the visiting national team(s).

evening session The last 1½ to 2 hours of play in a test or first-class match, starting immediately after tea break and ending with the draw of stumps.

exhibition match A match which is not part of any tournament or series, but played solely for the purpose of promoting cricket in the area or for raising funds. It is generally played between a visiting team and a local selection.

expensive A bowler or a bowling spell, conceding a higher number of runs as compared to the average scoring rate.

expert commentator A radio, or television commentator who discusses and analyses the technical aspects of the game (referred to as **expert comments**). Unlike a regular commentator who describes the ball by ball action, an expert commentator speaks

expert commentator

selectively, but with greater depth. He is usually a retired cricketer of repute who is able to draw upon his experience and knowledge in commenting upon the situation in the game, thus making it more interesting for the listeners.

express (express delivery) A fast bowler's delivery bowled with extra speed compared to his normal deliveries.

extra bounce The incremental height of a delivery after pitching, as compared to a delivery of normal height. Fast pitches tend to have a higher bounce, but some bowlers can also extract extra bounce on normal pitches by using their skills.

extra cover A fielding position about 20–25 yards from the batsman, between mid-off and cover. One of the busier positions on the off-side, it requires a high degree of agility in ground fielding to be able to field the powerful drives and ball placements on either side.

extra day When a match cannot be completed within the scheduled period due to bad weather or unplayable conditions, an extra day may be allowed for the game to continue to compensate for the time lost. This, however, is exceptional and may be allowed only if both teams and all concerned parties agree.

extra pace *(1)* Refers to a pitch helping fast bowlers, particularly at the start of the match when it is fresh and shiny. *(2)* An occasional delivery or short spell of higher than normal pace bowling under inspired conditions.

extra runs Additional run(s) conceded on a delivery due to misfield, overthrow or on account of extras.

extra slip A short term reinforcement of the slip cordon by the captain, by placing an additional slip fielder in anticipation of a catch or to put extra pressure on the batsman.

extra time Refers to the continuance of the game beyond the stipulated time, if allowed under the rules applicable in a match or tournament. Mainly followed in countries with longer daylight hours, the intent of this provision is to recover time lost due to unscheduled stoppage in play during the day.

extra(s) Run(s) not scored off the bat but added to the total on account of byes, leg-byes, wides and no-balls. See also *sundries.*

F f

face *(1)* A batsman ready to receive a bowler's delivery. *(2)* The front, flat side of a bat.

fall *(1)* Dismissal of a batsman. *(2)* Fall of a wicket.

fall of wickets Part of the scoresheet for an innings, showing the total score at the fall of each wicket. A completed innings records ten such entries.

far end Refers to the side of the ground or wickets, opposite the pavilion. Also referred to as the far side.

farm the bowling To play the bowling with ease and intelligence, scoring runs comfortably with singles and twos.

farm the strike (said of a batsman) To take a calculated single at the end of an over and retain strike, in order to ensure that the other (weaker) batting partner does not have to face a fresh over.

fast Denotes a high speed delivery or high speed bowling, in the normal context of the game.

fast bowler A bowler who specialises in bowling at a high speed; one who normally opens the team's bowling attack with a new ball. A genuine fast bowler of international class bowls at an average speed of about 80 miles an hour.

fast medium A bowler who's normal speed of bowling is higher than medium pace but slower than genuine fast bowling. A good fast medium bowler normally bowls at a speed of between 70 and 80 miles an hour.

fast outfield A ground where the ball travels quickly to the boundary, thus helping the batsmen to score boundaries more easily. The characteristics of a fast outfield are hard soil and trimmed grass, sometimes further accentuated by a marginal slope towards the boundary.

fast runner A batsman reputed for quick running between the wickets, along with good judgement for runs.

fast scoring A relative term meaning more runs scored in less time or from fewer balls/overs faced. In broad terms, scoring at an average rate of one run per ball in one-day cricket or one run per minute in the longer version, is considered a fast scoring rate.

fast wicket (fast track) A wicket on which the ball hurries after pitching, often with a higher bounce, thus helping fast bowlers. The test wicket at Perth (Australia) is reputed to be the fastest in the world.

faster one A delivery that is notably faster than the normal deliveries of a bowler; one intended to offer variation and surprise the batsman. See *quicker one*.

fastest fifty The achievement by a batsman of reaching a score of fifty in an innings with the least number of balls faced, as compared with any other batsmen during the entire tournament, or series. It applies to limited-over matches only and usually carries a cash award presented by a sponsor.

father of cricket W G Grace, a legendary right-handed all-rounder who dominated the English cricket scene between 1865 and 1908, is regarded as the father of cricket. Of a tall and hefty physique and sporting a long beard, Grace was immensely popular in the cricketing arena of those early times. He played first-class cricket for a record 43 years, scoring 54,896 runs with 126 centuries (avg 39.55), and capturing 2,876 wickets (avg 17.92 runs per wicket).

father of cricket

feather bed A slow or easy-paced wicket that offers little assistance to the bowlers. Although not conducive to attacking strokeplay, it allows batsmen to stay and compile runs. The test wicket at Kanpur, India, is known to be a feather bed wicket.

feed To continually bowl a similar type of delivery in the hope that the batsman will commit an error in playing a certain stroke and consequently be dismissed.

fence The circumference of the ground marked by a barrier, rope or fence;

commonly equated with the boundary line, although the boundary is often enclosed within the fence.

fend A half-hearted attempt by a batsman to play a rising delivery outside the off-stump, thus, either missing the ball completely or getting the outside edge of the bat.

festival match (carnival match) A match organised on the eve of a local festival or event, or purely for the purpose of exhibition and fund raising. One of the teams is typically a team visiting from another state or country, while the other one is a local ad hoc selection. The matches are played in a carnival-like atmosphere, with conditions greatly favouring the batsmen.

field *(1)* The entire oval shaped ground area on which the fielders are positioned; or the entire ground area within the periphery of the boundary line, excluding the pitch. *(2)* Fielders placed in a particular arrangement, e.g. attacking field, off-side field, etc.

field adjustment To move the fielders slightly to achieve a more precise field setting for a bowler who is ready to operate. See also *field change.*

field change A reshuffling of fielders at the start of a fresh over or during the over, sometimes due to a different batsman facing the bowling.

field placing/setting Refers to the deployment of fielders in specified positions. It is done by the captain in consultation with the bowler, taking note of the type of bowling, strengths/weaknesses of the batsman and game situation.

field restriction *(1)* The restriction in a one-day match on having no more than two fielders outside the thirty-yard circle. *(2)* The restriction in all first-class matches on having no more than two fielders on the leg-side, behind the square-leg umpire.

fielder (fieldsman) *(1)* Any player of the fielding side, other than the bowler or wicket-keeper. *(2)* A player positioned on the field for the purpose of stopping, catching, retrieving or throwing the ball.

fielding The action, or performance of a fielder or all the fielders collectively, in stopping, catching, retrieving or throwing the ball.

fielding

fielding position The name of a specific area or spot on the field, in relation to the batsman, e.g. slip, gully, mid-wicket, etc.

fielding side One of the two sides in a match, whose turn it is to bowl and field, while the other side bats.

fieldsman See *fielder.*

fifty A score of fifty or more runs (but less than one hundred) by a batsman. It is considered an individual batting milestone at all levels of the game.

final overs The last few overs of an innings in a one-day match notable for a change in playing strategy. Depending upon the situation, either more aggressive tactics may be employed to put pressure on the opposing side or a more cautious approach may be adopted to contain the damage.

fine *(1)* A prefix for fielding positions that are

fine

placed some what closer to the line of stumps, as compared to the normal positions, e.g. fine leg, fine third man. These positions are all behind the batsman, on either side of the wicket, and mainly intended to stop delicate cuts, glances or balls coming from the edge of the bat. *(2)* A delicate or edgy shot which deflects the ball behind the batsman and closer in line with the wickets, e.g. a fine leg glance.

fine leg An on-side fielding position behind the batsman, adjacent to long leg, about halfway to the boundary line.

finger (finger going up) As per the Laws of Cricket, the umpire declares a batsman out by pointing his fore finger upwards. The term thus refers to the umpire's finger going up to signal the end of a batsman's innings.

finger going up

finger-spin Turn given on a delivery mainly by imparting a forceful spin at the moment of delivery by the use of fingers.

finger-spinner A slow bowler who specialises in finger-spins, e.g. right-arm off-spinner or left-arm orthodox spinner.

fireworks A succession of cracking shots played by a batsman to score quick runs or to dominate the bowling.

first change The first bowler introduced into the attack, replacing one of the two bowlers who commenced the bowling operations at the start of an innings.

first-class match A match of three, or more days' duration, played between two teams of first-class status and recognised as such by the country's governing board of cricket. Matches between state or county cricket teams, playing in a nationally recognised tournament are typical examples of first-class matches. All test matches are also regarded as first-class.

first-class season A collective term for all the matches played during one cricketing year. In colder countries the first-class season starts at the beginning of summer, while in hotter countries it starts at the end of summer. Depending upon the amount of cricket played, each season may last from six to ten months.

first fifteen overs Refers to the first fifteen overs of a one-day match during which no more than two fielders can be placed outside the thirty-yard circle.

first-innings lead The excess runs scored by one side over the other side's first-innings total; applicable only for a match of two innings.

first slip An off-side fielding position behind the batsman and beside the wicket-keeper, but slightly deeper. Primarily a catching position to take catches coming off the outside edge of the bat, it is optionally deployed for spin but is a regular feature of a fast bowler's field setting.

five-day test A conventional test match scheduled to be played over five full days, as distinct from a shorter four-day test (long since discontinued), or an exceptional six-day test.

five-wicket haul Refers to the notable achievement of a bowler taking five or more wickets in an innings.

five wickets in an innings See *five-wicket haul.*

fiver A rare occurrence of five runs scored from a single delivery in either of two situations: *(i)* overthrows helping the batsman take additional runs, and *(ii)* the ball hitting an object (such as a helmet) left on the ground by the fielding side, thus resulting in five runs being awarded to the batsman.

fixture A scheduled match with teams, date(s) and venues firmly fixed.

fizzler A spinner's delivery that hurries through and goes straight after pitching. See *top-spinner.*

flash A quick, impulsive shot attempted or played to a ball passing outside the stump, by swinging the bat horizontally or at an angle. The shot often proves more risky than rewarding and is not recommended, except when going for quick runs.

flat delivery A fairly ordinary delivery by a spinner with little or no flight, and lacking turn as well.

flat hit A powerful shot played with a horizontal bat, hitting the ball in the front direction, between mid-off and mid-on.

flat surface A wicket offering no help to the bowlers; one where the ball comes at a comfortable pace and bounce after pitching, hence very favourable for batting.

flat throw A fast return by a fielder, sending the ball parallel to the ground.

flay Sustained aggressive batting, hitting the ball to all parts of the ground with power and ease.

flick An on-side stroke, ideally played off the front foot or on the rise, placing the ball over a wide arc between mid-wicket and backward square leg. The shot relies on crisp timing and firm wrist-work and is relatively safe as well as productive.

flick

flight The arc defined by a slow bowler's delivery, from the moment it leaves his hand, until it lands. A flighted delivery initially propels the ball up above the bowler's hand, before it gradually descends to land in front of the batsman. Flight compliments spin (just as line compliments length) and constitutes a critical success factor for spin bowling.

flighted delivery/ball A delivery bowled with flight, as opposed to a flat or fast delivery.

flipper A variation delivery in the armoury of a wrist spinner. Delivered from the back of the hand, a flipper goes faster and straighter after pitching, thus deceiving the batsman who may expect it to turn.

floater A spinner's delivery b^wled with a prominent use of his palms (rather than fingers) to flight and turn the ball.

floor (floor a catch) To drop a not too difficult catch after getting it into the hand(s).

fly slip An unorthodox fielding position on the off-side, deeper than the normal slips and closer to short third man. More suitable for one-day games than for the longer version, the function of the fly slip is to stop singles, as well as catch a batsman who is attempting late cuts, or slices.

follow-on *(1)* A situation wherein the team conceding a large first-innings deficit is asked by the opposing captain to continue batting and play the second innings immediately. The extent of deficit that gives rise to a follow-on option depends upon the length of the match; e.g., a minimum deficit of 150 runs is necessary for a three- or four-day match, and a 200 run deficit for a five-day match. *(2)* The second innings played by a team immediately after its first, upon being asked to do so by the opposing captain.

follow-through *(1 bowling)* The continuation of a bowler's action with deceleration after the ball is delivered. *(2 batting)* The continuation of the body and bat movement to bring it to a balanced and graceful stop after the stroke is played.

foot stop The action of a fielder to intercept a speeding ball with his foot.

foothold The area of the pitch around the bowling and popping crease where the bowlers land their feet at the moment of delivery.

footwork Movement and positioning of feet when playing any stroke. Good footwork implies the use of very skilful and graceful feet movements to get into the precise position to execute shots.

force A controlled straight-bat shot, sending the ball to the deep while maintaining the safety of defence. Played on both sides of the wicket, it relies on good timing and a short push of the arms to impart power into the shot.

force the pace A conscious attempt by a batsman to increase the rate of scoring; to be predisposed to playing forceful shots, as well as taking quick runs through intelligent ball placement.

forcing shot A straight-bat shot, halfway between a drive and a push. Mostly played in front of the wickets, its purpose is to hit the ball deeper, while maintaining the safety and elegance of a straight-bat stroke.

forcing shot

forfeit The complete surrender of an innings or match by one or both teams. This rare situation arises when the playing time is severely cut short due to any reason and both sides agree to seek a result within the available time. A match may be forfeited if one team does not show up on time or stays away in protest. .

form A player's performance over a period of several innings or matches, demonstrating quality of play as well as runs scored or wickets taken.

forward A modified fielding position which is slightly forward of square on either side of the wicket, e.g. forward point or forward square leg.

forward stroke Any stroke played by stretching the front foot to the pitch of the ball.

four A score of four runs resulting from the ball crossing the boundary line. Also known as fourer.

four-day test A test match played over four days instead of the normal five days. Such test matches were in vogue until the 1960s, and were played mainly between a stronger and a weaker team, but have long since been discontinued.

free hit A cracking shot to a loose delivery, placing the ball comfortably in an unmanned area.

free hit area A wide gap in the field where a batsman's hit can fetch easy runs. A free hit area is often deliberately created by the fielding captain to entice and trap the batsman.

French cut A misconnected off-side shot that deflects the ball unintentionally from the inner edge of the bat to fine leg or backward square-leg area.

friendly match A specially arranged match, the purpose of which is either to give the teams playing experience or simply to stage cricket at the nominated venue; a match which is not a part of any series, league or tournament.

front cut A cut shot played off the front foot, as different from the normal back-foot position. The ball affording such a shot is generally short of length, and goes outside the off-stump.

front foot The foot of the batsman that is closer or visible to the bowler as the batsman faces a delivery. Proper use of the front foot is an important element of batting technique and all forward strokes are played by moving it to the pitch of the ball.

front-foot drive

front-foot drive A stroke played by thrusting the front foot forward and striking the ball in front with a full flow of the bat, which is held straight throughout the motion. Depending upon the delivery, the stroke can be played anywhere between cover and mid-wicket.

front-foot regulation The current no-ball rule wherein a no-ball is declared if the bowler's foot crosses the popping crease at the time of delivery.

front-foot strokes Strokes played by moving the front foot towards the pitch of the ball.

frontline The top order batsmen, or bowlers in a team, who get into action in the early part of an innings.

full member Refers to a test-playing country, with full ICC membership. Currently there are ten full member countries, namely: Australia, Bangladesh, England, India, New Zealand, Pakistan, Sri Lanka, South Africa, West Indies and Zimbabwe.

full pitch A delivery that is considerably over-pitched, which the batsman is easily able to play as full toss. It is normally considered a loose delivery, being easier to negotiate or hit for runs.

full series A series involving five test matches, with or without the one-day international matches, which are considered a separate sub-set of the series.

full toss A delivery that reaches the batsman without pitching; also considered a loose delivery, as it allows the batsman enough time to take a powerful hit.

fumble Imprecise fielding, resulting in the ball popping out of the hands of the fielder.

G g

gap Space between two fielders which neither of them can cover easily.

gardening A casual tapping, cleaning or mending of the pitch by the batsman, during the short intervals of time between deliveries or overs.

gate Idiomatic expression for the space left between bat and pad when the batsman plays a stroke. Correct batting technique advocates complete avoidance of the creation of such space when playing a stroke so that the ball does not pass through and cause a dismissal.

gentleman's game Cricket is considered a gentleman's game as it imbibes many gentlemanly attributes, like formal attire, total acceptance of the umpire's decisions, respect for the captain's orders, etc.

Gentlemen Refers to the classification of amateur cricketers, as distinct from professional cricketers (Players), that existed in England until 1962. Amateur cricketers played the game as a hobby and were not entitled to receive any match fees and were hence referred to as the Gentlemen. Matches between a selection of Gentlemen and Players were a regular feature of the English cricket season from the early nineteenth century until abolished in 1962.

genuine all-rounder An all-rounder so proficient in batting as well as bowling that his selection can be justified on the basis of any one skill; a player whose inclusion in the side effectively gives it one additional bowler or batsman. Some of the best all-rounders in test cricket were, Gary Sobers (West Indies), Ian Botham (England), Imran Khan (Pakistan) and Kapil Dev (India).

get out A batsman dismissed, or team being all out. The term is generally used when describing the manner of dismissal.

get the eye in Said of a batsman who bats cautiously at the start of his innings to get a good feel of the bowling and the nature of the wicket.

give the ball air A spinner's delivery imparting extra flight, so that the ball remains in the air longer than usual. It adds variety to the bowling and also entices the batsman to play bold shots.

given out An appeal for dismissal upheld by the umpire under dubious circumstances. See also *doubtful decision.*

giving it a charge Said of a batsman who steps out of his crease, as the bowler is delivering the ball, with the intention of playing an attacking shot in front of the wickets.

giving width (giving room) To bowl far outside the off-stump, allowing the batsman an easy opportunity to swing the bat freely and play an attacking shot on the off-side.

glance A straight-bat stroke played by turning the face of the bat at the precise moment of contact with the ball, so that it rolls off smoothly on its own momentum. The more popular glance is the one played on the leg-side, called leg glance. A similar stroke on the off-side is usually referred to as a glide.

glaze ball A new cricket ball with a hard and shining surface.

glide An off-side stroke played with the bat held straight and firmly angled, so that the ball deflects finely on its own momentum. The stroke is typically played between backward point and third man on the off-side.

glove a catch A catch coming off the batsman's gloves, rather than off the bat.

gloveman (glovesman) See *wicket-keeper.*

gloves

gloves Refers to the padded gloves worn by a batsman or a wicket-keeper to protect the fingers from being injured by the ball.

go for shots To bat aggressively with the aim of scoring runs quickly.

going out A delivery moving away from the batsman from leg to off, either in the air or after pitching.

golden arm Said of an occasional bowler who manages to capture a wicket or two at an important stage of the game when the other regular bowlers fail to do so.

golden duck A batsman out without scoring to the first ball he receives. If the performance is repeated in the second innings, it is called a golden double duck or a golden pair.

golden pair A batsman out for duck to the first ball he receives in both innings of a match. Also referred to as a king pair or a golden double duck.

good arm Said of a fielder who is reputed for sending fast and accurate returns.

good call A quick run completed just in time as the throw comes in. It demonstrates excellent rapport between the two batsmen, with one batsman calling the run and the other responding quickly.

good decision A correct decision given by the umpire in a tense or controversial situation.

good length The ideal spot for a bowler to pitch his delivery. For the batsman, a ball pitched in this area causes the maximum difficulty in playing an attacking shot. The good length spot varies according to the type of bowler, as well as the type of batsman or wicket.

good runner A batsman who is an excellent runner between the wickets in terms of speed, judgement for runs and coordination with his batting partner.

good start An appreciable progress recorded by a side early in the match; e.g., a batting side putting up a decent score with few wickets lost or a bowling side capturing a few early wickets. In one-day games, the rate of scoring also indicates whether a team has had a good start to its innings.

good toss to lose The advantage of winning a toss is sometimes in doubt because of uncertainty as to how the wicket will play. Losing the toss in such a situation puts the onus of decision making on the opposing captain and is, therefore, said to be a 'good toss to lose'.

good toss to win Refers to the advantage a captain has in either electing to bat, if it is a good batting wicket or electing to bowl, if the wicket offers assistance to bowlers. Hence, winning the toss in this situation is termed 'a good toss to win'.

googly A delivery by a right-arm leg-spin bowler that turns like an off-break upon pitching; also described as an off-spin with a leg-spin action. Googlies often surprise batsmen who may play them for normal leg-spin.

grains The natural vertical lines on the blade of a cricket bat, indicative of the good quality of wood (willow) used in its manufacture.

grass *(1)* The green outfield, outside the pitch area. *(2)* To drop a catch.

greasy wicket See *wet pitch*.

green light A not out decision given by the third umpire after watching television replays and communicated by switching on a green light.

green pitch (green top) A wicket with some amount of grass sprouting on the surface. It is helpful to fast bowlers as the ball skids and bounces upon pitching. Not surprisingly, batsmen do not relish playing on a green pitch.

grip The manner of holding a bat or ball, for batting, or bowling.

batting grip

ground In technical terms, the entire field on which the game is played, but excluding the pitch. In general terms it includes all the constructions attached to the field.

ground equipment A composite term for all the tools, machinery and facilitation items used on a cricket ground, such as, lawn mowers, rollers, movable sight-screens, etc.

ground fielding The skill and efficiency of a player/team, in stopping, retrieving and returning balls, to deny or reduce run scoring opportunities for the batsmen.

ground shot A stroke that sends the ball along the ground. The term more aptly describes shots hit into the deep field, rather than those played close to the wicket.

ground staff Employees engaged in the provision and maintenance of playing facilities at the ground.

grounding the bat Refers to a batsman's action of thrusting the bat along the ground when completing a run. An elementary aspect of proper running, it is particularly important when the batsman is entering the popping crease to beat a fielder's return.

groundsman A person responsible for the preparation of the ground, particularly the wicket. Referred to in some countries as curator.

guard A marked position in front of the stumps where the batsman takes stance. The marking is done with chalk, or by rubbing the toe of the bat, after checking the correct position with the umpire. The three common markings or guards, are **leg guard** (in line with the leg stump), **middle guard** (in line with the middle stump), and **leg and middle guard** (between leg and middle stumps). Batsmen seldom take the **off guard** (in line with the off-stump) as it increases the chances of being out lbw.

gully A close catching and fielding position on the off-side, between third slip and point; commonly employed for pace bowlers attacking the off-stump, because the away movement of deliveries or strokes played with an angled bat, tend to carry the ball to this position.

Hh

hairline decision A very close run out or stumping situation decided upon by the third umpire after much study and deliberation of the slow motion action replays.

half-century (half-ton) An individual score of fifty or more runs (but less than one hundred) made by a batsman; considered a measure of batting success at all levels of the game. See *fifty*.

half-cock A defensive stroke played by moving only half forward, rather than fully stretched forward, to a ball pitching on good length or just short of good length. The bat is held straight and angled down when playing the stroke to smother the turn and bounce of the delivery.

half-hit A lofted shot that fails to carry the full distance due to imperfect timing or inadequate power, and lands short of the deep field positions. The typical half-hit areas are in front of the wicket, between wide mid-off and wide mid-on.

half-volley A delivery pitched well up to the batsman, allowing an easy hit off the front foot just as the ball bounces up after pitching.

hall of fame The famous hall at the Lord's Cricket Ground, London, where photographs of great cricketers and numerous other cricketing artefacts are displayed.

handle The long cylindrical part of the bat, connecting the blade, used to grip the bat. It is made of several layers of cane and rubber which absorb the shock when the ball is hit. For additional security and comfort, the handle is also wrapped with twine and covered with a rubber sleeve.

handled the ball A very unusual form of dismissal for a batsman. As per the Laws of Cricket (no. 33), 'either batsman on appeal shall be out Handled The Ball if he wilfully touches the ball while in play with the hand not holding the bat unless he does so with the consent of the opposite side.' The bowler does not get credit for a 'handled the ball' dismissal.

hang A delivery that appears to hold back after pitching or bounces slower than expected. Bowled by skilful use of spin and flight, it can cause the batsman to mistime a stroke or be beaten.

hang the bat A tentative stroke played to a rising delivery outside the off-stump, often failing to make contact with the ball or edging it at best. Although the bat is held straight when playing this stroke, it is kept away from the body and lacks power and balance.

hang the gloves Idiomatic expression meaning to retire from active cricket. To 'hang the gloves' means to put the gloves away, with no intention of using them for cricket.

harrow bat A bat smaller than normal in size meant for use by younger players.

hat-trick The rare feat of a bowler taking three wickets from three consecutive deliveries, which need not be in the same over but must be in the same match.

haul A good number of wickets taken by a bowler during an innings, match, tournament or season, as stated.

heartbeat graph A line graph that plots the average scoring rate of a team's innings at the end of every over in a one-day match. Generated with the aid of a computer program, it is used to study the progressive as well as the comparative scoring rates of the two teams at various stages of the match.

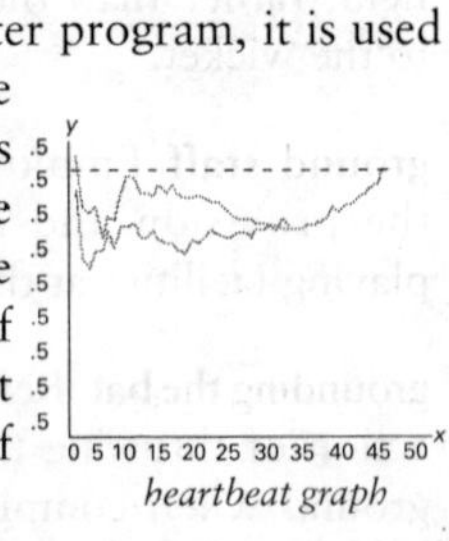

heartbeat graph

heavy bat A bat weighing close to, or slightly exceeding the outer limit of 48 ounces. Although there is no statutory limit on how heavy a bat should be, the normal range is between 36 and 48 ounces.

heavy roller One of the two types of metallic rollers used to firm up the pitch before commencement of an innings. See *roller.*

helmet A cap made of fibre glass or similar hard material, worn by batsmen to protect the head against the rising deliveries of fast bowlers; also used by leg-side close-in fielders.

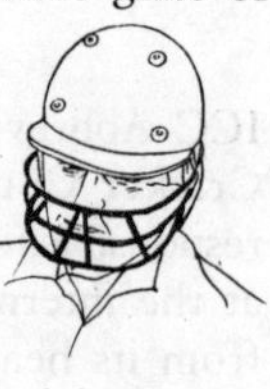
helmet

high-arm action A bowler's individual style of bowling with the ball delivered from a maximum overhead position, thus helping achieve some extra bounce. The body posture is also relatively erect through run up and final delivery when bowling with a high-arm action.

high catch A shot sent towering into the air, but resulting in a catch in the outfield.

high catch

high-scoring game A match in which batsmen dominate the play and both teams score large totals.

highest Refers to the batsman's best score or the maximum total registered by a team, in a single innings during the stated period—tournament, series, season, career, etc.

hit A powerful and well connected shot, played with greater intent on aggression than safety or correctness of stroke; commonly employed when in pursuit of quick runs.

hit-and-run A situation when the batsmen are intent on scoring runs off almost every ball to increase the total. This situation occurs mainly towards the end of the innings in a one-day match.

hit the ball twice An unusual mode of dismissal wherein a batsman is declared out if he wilfully strikes the ball a second time with his bat or person, except for the sole purpose of guarding his wicket.

hit wicket A mode of dismissal in which the wickets are disturbed (bails coming off) with the bat or any part of a batsman's person or equipment, in the process of playing a delivery or setting off for a run.

hitter A batsman predominantly inclined to play attacking shots, regardless of the type of bowling or the game situation.

hoick An agressive cross-batted shot, hitting the ball to the deep field on the leg side; similar to a pull, but lacking in proper footwork and elegance.

hoist A powerful shot, hitting the ball high into the deep field on the on-side or in front of the batsman. A typical hoisted shot is played off the front foot, picking the ball up on the half-volley and sending it to the ropes between mid-on and mid-wicket.

holdall See *cricket bag.*

hole out To hit a lofted shot that results in a catch being taken in the deep field.

home *(1)* Ground belonging to or within the territory of, the host team.

(2) Space between the popping crease and the wickets, where a batsman is positioned when playing a delivery. It is also the place a batsman reaches to complete a run.

home and dry/easy Said of a batsman completing the run comfortably, i.e. reaching the popping crease well in time, before the ball is received from the fielder.

hook An audacious stroke played by swinging the bat horizontally against a rising delivery pitched short of good length. A well connected hook shot dispatches the ball to the deep leg-side field, anywhere between mid-wicket and fine leg. Often a batsman's bold answer to a bumper, the shot is spectacular to watch, but also carries the risk of dismissal through a catch.

hook

hostile wicket A pitch where the ball rises quickly and awkwardly upon landing, thus exposing the batsmen to injury; or a pitch with extra pace and awkward bounce, which is helpful to fast bowlers but difficult for batting.

howzaat The standard appeal by a bowler or fielders, asking the umpire 'how's that'. It implies that the fielding side believes a dismissal has been achieved and requests the umpire to uphold it. In reality there are far more appeals than dismissals, and 'howzaat' is often shouted at the top of the voice rather than quietly appealed.

howzhee A variation of a *howzaat* appeal, asking the umpire 'how is he' and requesting that the batsman be declared out.

hundred A century, i.e. a score of a hundred, or more runs by an individual batsman. It is a batting landmark at all levels of the game, particularly so at the higher levels.

hustle A pace bowler's delivery that skids or hastens after pitching, making it difficult for the batsman to negotiate. While a lively pitch is conducive to such bowling, it also requires skilful delivery by the bowler to make it effective.

I i

ICC Abbreviation for 'International Cricket Council', the organisation responsible for governance of the game at the international level. Operating from its headquarters located at the Lord's Cricket Ground, London, the ICC currently has ten full members (test-playing countries) and more than twenty associate members (non-test-playing countries).

ICC Knock-out Also known as the 'mini world cup', this is a tournament of one-day matches played on a knock-out basis between the ICC full-member countries. It is played once every two years, and is staged outside the participating countries with a view to popularising the game in other major cricket following countries. The first such tournament was held in Malaysia in 1998 and won by South Africa.

improvised stroke A variation of an orthodox stroke, aiming to place the ball in the gaps for runs; usually played when the batsman is attempting to score quick runs or when confident and well set.

in-cutter See *off-cutter.*

in the middle Batsman at the crease; a batsman who is not out and is continuing to bat.

independent umpire See *neutral umpire.*

indoor cricket *(1)* Refers to cricket facilities provided in a covered shed, so that the game can be practised in a compact and protected area; ideal for cricket practice in late evenings and during inclement weather. *(2)* A mini version of the game played (albeit less seriously), in a warehouse measuring 10 metres by 30 metres, with net, or wall protection all around. The game is played with a softer ball and several ad hoc rules are specially agreed to. The number of players is limited to eight on each side.

infield Part of the field which is within a 20 to 30 yard distance from the batsman, as opposed to the deep field or mid-field.

injudicious stroke A stroke wrongly selected for the type of delivery or situation, resulting in dismissal or undue risk being taken by the batsman.

inner edge (inside edge) *(1)* The edge of the bat that is closer to the batsman. *(2)* A misconnected shot deflecting the ball off the inside edge in a direction entirely different – usually on the leg-side – from what was intended.

inner gloves Plain, cotton gloves worn inside the wicket-keeping gloves for additional comfort, improved grip and sweat absorption. Also referred to as inners.

inners See *inner gloves.*

innings *(1)* The turn of an individual player to bat in a match. *(2)* The turn of a team to bat, as opposed to field or bowl. In both cases, the performance is measured by the number of runs scored—with or without being dismissed in the former case, and by the number of wickets lost in the latter.

innings defeat/victory The result in a two innings match wherein the first-innings total of one team exceeds the other's aggregate score for both innings. The winning team, therefore, records an 'innings victory' without having to play its second innings, while the other suffers an 'innings defeat'.

innovative shot A novel and unorthodox batting stroke, but effective and well executed.

inside edge See *inner edge.*

inside out An improvised cover drive, played with the batsman turning his body and moving into the line of the ball to generate extra power and momentum; played with a full flow of the bat, hitting the ball in the deep and wide cover region.

inswing A fast or medium fast delivery that deviates in the air from the off- to on-side of the wicket. The bowler uses a special grip, with a slight modification of the bowling action, to get the ball to inswing. An ideal inswing delivery **(inswinger)** comes in to the batsman from just outside the off-stump. See also *outswing.*

inswinging yorker (incoming yorker) A fast delivery, combining an inswing with a yorker (see *yorker*); particularly effective against new batsmen or when bowled as a surprise weapon to a well settled batsmen.

intercepting The action of a fielder in stopping a ball that is speeding away from him.

international cricket calendar Schedule of test and one-day matches to be played between the major cricket-playing nations over a given period.

International Cricket Council See *ICC*.

international rating Refers to the officially published rankings for national teams and individual players, based upon performances during the current calendar year or the preceding twelve months. Calculated separately for tests and one-day international matches, the rankings are measured on a points scale which is regularly updated. The top ten under each category – teams, batsmen, bowlers, etc. – are periodically published by the media.

international umpire An umpire who is nominated by his country to be on the ICC panel of twenty international umpires. For test matches, it is mandatory to have one of these umpires (also called a neutral umpire) to be officiating in the match, together with one national or local umpire.

interruption A temporary and unscheduled stoppage in play due to any reason, like bad weather, ball replacement, a problem with the spectators, etc.

intimidation Persistent bowling of fast, short-pitched deliveries, intended to cause injury to the batsman; bowling with a strategy to dismiss the batsman by causing him to commit errors in an attempt to avoid injury.

Irish swing Movement of the ball in the direction opposite to that intended by the bowler or anticipated by the batsman.

it's not cricket The game of cricket imbibes a tradition of fairness and the sporting spirit. To break these values is considered to be against the spirit of the game and hence, 'not cricket'.

J j

jab A hurried, off-side stroke played at the last moment to fend off the ball.

juggle To catch or field the ball after several attempts.

juicy A very easy delivery, allowing the batsman to take a free hit into a vacant area.

junior cricket Matches/tournaments played below the first-class level, generally comprising local teams representing private clubs, commercial organisations and educational institutions.

K k

keep low A delivery that does not rise to the expected height after pitching, thus making it difficult for the batsman to play.

keep one's end up Said of a batsman who plays a major, responsible knock, while wickets are falling at the other end.

keeper See *wicket-keeper.*

kick A delivery that jumps up unexpectedly after pitching, thus making it difficult for the batsman to negotiate.

king pair A batsman out for duck to the first ball he receives, in both the innings of a match. Also referred to as a golden pair.

kit A very large bag containing an individual player's or team's cricketing equipment, like bats, pads, gloves, balls, etc.

knock *(1)* A team's turn to bat. *(2)* An individual batsman's innings, particularly when he achieves a decent score. *(3)* To practice batting by knocking the ball around.

knock-down To be comprehensively beaten and bowled with one or more stumps actually falling to the ground.

knock-out A tournament, or a stage thereof, in which the team losing a match is eliminated from the tournament.

kookaburra A special type of cricket ball commonly used in Australia. It has a flatter seam and is made of tougher leather to suit the hard wickets found there.

L 1

large ground For a ground of normal size, the boundary line is, on an average, 75 yards from the centre of the pitch (the statutory limit is 60 yards minimum and 90 yards maximum). A large ground, therefore, is one where the average distance from the pitch to the boundary line is over 75 yards, e.g. Eden Gardens, Calcutta and the Melbourne Cricket Ground commonly known as MCG.

last man The last batsman to come in to bat in a team's innings, i.e. number eleven, or nine down batting position.

last man out The last wicket to fall in an innings. Scoreboards normally display the individual score of the last batsman out, as well as the total score at that stage.

last over Refers to the last over of a bowler's quota or the final over of the innings in a one-day match. The latter often produces dramatic events, with the batting side trying to score runs and the bowling side trying to contain runs, or dismiss the batsmen.

last wicket pair Partnership for the tenth wicket of an innings, with dismissal of either of the two batsmen resulting in the team being all out.

late call A somewhat belated signal by one batsman to the other to take a run.

late cut A variation of the cut shot played a split second later than normal, after the ball has just passed the off-stump. Unlike the conventional cut, which is a robust one, the late cut relies on delicate timing and wrist work. The bat is also brought down over the ball in an elegant manner, instead of with a powerful swing as for the other cut shots.

late order The lower half of a team's batting line-up, mostly comprising players (bowlers) who are less known for their batting skills.

late swing A delivery that starts to deviate in the air at the later stage of its trajectory, i.e. when it is closer to the batsman. A late swing delivery is more difficult for the batsman to negotiate as it leaves him very little time to adjust the stroke.

Laws of Cricket Refers to the official set of laws (numbers 1 to 42, with various sub-clauses) which govern all aspects of the game. These laws are issued by the ICC and are followed uniformly all over the world, at all levels of the game. Only the ICC has the power to modify or amend any of these laws, but such amendments/ modifications have been few and far between over the years in order to maintain consistency and uniformity. (Note: It has not been possible to identify exactly when the laws were formulated. The bulk of them, obviously, evolved during the nineteenth century and were already in vogue when the first-ever test match was played in 1877. The ICC was formed in 1909 and must have officially adopted the laws a little later.)

lbw Abbreviation for Leg Before Wicket. See *leg before wicket*.

lead *(1)* The difference in the totals of the two teams at a given stage of the game. *(2)* To be the captain of a side.

leading arm The non-bowling arm of a bowler which moves ahead of the bowling arm when sending down a delivery.

leading edge The far edge of the bat (the one facing the bowler) when turning or flicking a delivery to the leg-side.

league A round-robin tournament in which all participating teams play against one another and the team winning the most matches or scoring the highest number of points, is declared the winner.

league match A match forming a part of a round-robin tournament.

lean patch A prolonged period of non-performance by a player due to loss of form, bad luck, or both.

leather The cricket ball which is made of leather.

leather hunt Complete dominance of the batsmen over bowlers during a session or innings, with fielders having to continuously chase the ball (leather) all over the field.

leave A delivery that moves away from the batsman after pitching, to outside the off-stump; more commonly bowled by pace bowlers using swing, seam or cut techniques.

leave the ball alone Batsman watching the delivery pass through to the wicket-keeper, without attempting to play it.

leaving the batsman See *outgoing delivery*.

left-arm (left-armer) A bowler who sends down deliveries with his left-hand, bowling either spin or pace.

left-arm orthodox spin The conventional type of spin bowling by a left-arm spinner, with the ball turning from leg to off for a right-handed batsman. Spin is imparted by the use of fingers (rather than wrist), like for right-arm off-spin bowling. Also referred to as *slow left-arm*.

left-hander's gloves The special batting gloves which suit the grip of a left-handed batsman.

lefty A left-handed batsman or bowler.

leg *(1)* One half of the pitch or ground, on the batsman's leg-side. *(2)* Area of the pitch on or outside the leg stump. See *leg-side*.

leg before wicket (lbw; leg before) One of the common modes of dismissal, but also the most complex and controversial. In simpler terms, a batsman is declared out lbw if the ball hits any part of his body (except the hands), instead of hitting the wicket. The umpire considers a number of technical points in making his judgement on an lbw appeal.

leg-break A spinner's delivery that turns from leg- to off-side of the wicket. See *leg-spin*.

leg-bye Runs scored when the ball deflects off the batsman's body or pads, rather than off the bat or gloves, as he misses playing a delivery. Such runs are not credited to the batsman, but added to extras. Leg-byes are, however, not allowed if the batsman deliberately uses his body or pads to deflect the ball.

umpire's signal for leg-bye

leg-cutter A fast delivery moving from leg- to off-side upon pitching. It is bowled by fast or medium fast bowlers by adopting a special grip and giving the ball a 'cut' at the moment of delivery.

leg glance A delicate, wristy stroke in which the ball is deflected behind the batsman's legs, by turning the bat at the precise moment of contact. A very safe yet productive stroke, it can be played off the front or back foot, ideally to balls pitched on or outside the leg stump.

leg glance

leg guard *(i)* A stance position with the bat covering the leg stump and feet positioned outside the leg stump. *(ii)* An obsolete term for pads.

leg-gully A leg-side close-in fielding position behind the batsman, between short backward square leg and leg slip. It is the leg-side equivalent of the gully, but rarely used as the bowling attack is mainly concentrated on the off-side.

leg hit A powerful shot played on the leg-side. The expression more aptly describes shots that are other than conventional ones like hook, pull, or sweep.

leg-side The same as on-side; however, the term 'leg-side' is generally used when referring to field placing, whereas 'on-side' is used in relation to batting strokes.

leg slip A leg-side fielding position, nearly the mirror image of first slip, i.e. behind the batsman and beside the wicket-keeper. It is mainly deployed to catch balls deflecting off the inside edge of the bat when the bowler is attacking the leg stump. The practical use of this position is, however, becoming rare due to fielding restrictions on the leg-side.

leg-spin Turn imparted on the ball, causing it to deviate from leg- to off-side upon pitching. The turn is imparted by finger or wrist action (or both) at the moment of delivery.

grip for bowling a leg spin

leg-spinner A bowler specialising in the art of leg-spin bowling. A conventional leg-spinner is one who bowls right-arm leg-breaks to a right-handed batsman.

leg stump The last of the three wooden rods that comprise the wickets, as viewed from the off-side. See *stumps*.

leg theory A bowling strategy to attack the batsman's leg stump with a packed leg-side field. Practised to good effect during the early thirties (the bodyline series), it was considered negative and leg-side field restrictions were subsequently introduced to control excessive use of this kind of strategy.

leg trap Refers to the placement of two, or more, fielders in close catching positions on the leg-side, like leg slip, forward short-leg and backward short-leg. Setting a leg-trap field is not very common and is mainly deployed when a spinner is attacking the batsman's leg stump on a turning wicket.

leg umpire One of the two umpires officiating in the game from the square-leg position. He is mainly responsible for adjudicating the run out and stumping decisions. At the end of each over, the leg umpire moves to perform the main umpire's duties, and vice-versa. See *umpire.*

leggie (leggy) A right-arm leg-spin bowler.

length A measure of bowling accuracy in respect of where the ball lands on the pitch. A ball pitching closer to the batsman is termed full length, while one pitching about halfway down the pitch is termed short-pitch or long hop. A bowler normally tries to bowl deliveries at a good length spot.

length ball A ball that comes up to the batsman after pitching around the good length area.

let-off A chance given to the batsman due to errors committed by the fielding side.

life *(1)* An opportunity for dismissal missed by the fielding side or a fortuitous extension to the batsman's innings due to faulty fielding. *(2)* Quality of pitch in terms of the assistance it provides fast bowlers.

lift *(1)* To play a lofted shot into the deep field. *(2)* Extra bounce in the delivery after pitching, achieved either due to greater force exerted by the bowler or due to the type of wicket.

light Refers to the condition of light on the ground, which should be adequate for the game to be played safely. In certain situations, the game may continue despite inadequate light if both the captains agree to play. See also *bad light.*

light bat A normal cricket bat weighs between 36 and 48 ounces. A light bat is one which weighs in the lower range, around 36-40 ounces.

light roller One of the two types of metallic rollers (heavy, or light) used to firm up the pitch. See *roller.*

limited-overs cricket/matches Refers to all such matches in which each side plays only one innings, limited to a specified number of overs. The matches are scheduled to be completed within a day, hence also referred to as one-day matches or a shorter version of the game. Certain special rules are applicable to this form of cricket.

line Direction of a delivery in relation to the stumps. Along with length, line is one of the two basic attributes of good bowling. Bowling on the stumps, or just outside, is considered the ideal line in most situations.

line of attack A planned spell of bowling in which the bowler persistently pitches the ball around a particular spot, in an attempt to contain the batsman, or force him to make an error, e.g. bowling outswingers on the off-stump.

line-up The order in which a team's players are expected to go in to bat; or simply, the list of players in a team known for their batting skills.

lively pace Nippy and effective fast bowling, with extra zeal and energy put in by the bowler.

lob A poorly played stroke resulting in the ball ballooning up or going high up in the air, to the close-in or mid-field area.

local six A lofted shot that results in a catch in the deep, but humorously described as a possible six at another (local) ground.

loft A shot played in the air towards the deep field; mostly refers to high shots played off the front foot.

lofted drive A front-foot or back-foot drive, hitting the ball high into the deep field.

lolly A very easy catch. See also *dolly.*

long A prefix for certain fielding positions, indicating placement of a fielder closer to the boundary, e.g. long-on or long-off.

long batting line-up A side containing several players reputed for their batting skills (e.g. all-rounders or wicket-keeper), in addition to the regular number of specialist batsmen.

long boundary Boundary positions that are relatively longer than other positions on the same ground or longer compared to any normal ground, e.g. the long-on or long-off boundary may be longer than the mid-wicket boundary.

long field A segment of the deep field behind the bowler, extending from wide long-off to wide long-on.

Long Hall A famous, long room at the Lord's cricket ground, London, housing photographs and mementoes of the game's famous personalities and special events.

long handle Refers to a modified grip by the batsman, holding the bat higher up the handle to generate greater swing and power for hitting shots. Thus, expressions like **using the long handle** or **giving it a long handle** mean that the batsman is inclined to attack the bowling.

long hop A very short pitched delivery that comes up to the batsman at an easy pace and height, allowing him to score a free hit.

long leg A leg-side fielding position near the boundary line, between fine leg and backward square leg.

long-off An off-side fielding position near the boundary line, anywhere between deep extra cover and straight in front of the batsman.

long-on An on-side fielding position near the boundary line, anywhere between deep wide mid-on and straight in front of the batsman.

long over An over in which several extra deliveries are bowled due to the bowler sending down wides and/or no-balls.

long run-up A fast bowler's run-up of, say, fifteen yards or more; a bowler's run up that seems longer than necessary for his style of bowling.

long slip A modified slip position, a few yards deeper and wider than usual, and almost merging with short third man.

long stop A fielding position behind the wicket-keeper, used as a second line of defence to stop byes and edgy shots. This position is, however, seldom used in modern day cricket.

long tail A side having many players (mainly bowlers) with poor batting skills, who are not expected to contribute much to the team's total.

long tour An overseas tour lasting six weeks, or more, during which five tests and several other matches are played on the side, in addition to three or more one-day internationals.

longer version of the game Matches that are played with two innings per side and not limited by the number of overs per innings. The term mainly refers to test and first-class matches.

loop The deceptive curve and drop in a flighted delivery that makes it difficult for the batsman to judge the pitch of the ball. Existence of an effective loop in the delivery often distinguishes a good spinner from an ordinary one.

loose delivery A harmless ball, lacking in length or direction, and presenting the batsman with an easy scoring opportunity.

loose shot A half-hearted or improperly executed stroke, getting the batsman into trouble or resulting in a scoring opportunity not being maximised.

loosener The initial deliveries of a new bowler, bowled mainly to loosen the body and get a feel of the line/length before he settles down to bowl more seriously.

Lord's The oldest cricket ground in England, famous for staging numerous historic cricketing events: the first ever first-class cricket match in 1814, the decisive final test of the first Ashes series played in England in 1884, the finals of the 1975, 1979, 1983 and 1999 world cups, etc. Situated in London, Lord's is also home to the famous Marleborne Cricket Club, the head office of the ICC, and houses a unique cricket museum. Although not very large, the ground is picturesque and well maintained and has long been regarded the Mecca of cricket. It was constructed in 1810 by Thomas Lord, at the behest of his local cricket club, and is named after him.

lost ball A situation during a match when the ball is lost in play and cannot be retrieved. In such situations a replacement ball may be used, if requested by the bowling side, with six runs added to the batsman's, or extras account, if not scored already. A lost ball situation rarely occurs in first-class cricket as the grounds have adequate barriers all around.

low catch Ball coming off the bat at a low height and caught inches from the ground. Low catches are mostly taken by the wicket-keeper or in positions closer to the wicket.

low-scoring game A match in which bowlers have ascendancy over batsmen and both teams fail to score high enough totals, resulting in the aggregate runs scored in the match being very much below average.

lower order batsmen Batsmen who go in to bat after five or six wickets have fallen, particularly the tail-enders batting at number 9 to 11 batting positions.

lower trajectory A slightly quicker delivery of a spinner, bowled without flight, and aimed to pitch around the good length spot.

lowest score A measure of a batsman's, or a team's, weakest batting performance in the stated level of cricket.

lucky Said of a player who benefits from a faulty judgement by the umpire or errors committed by the opposing side or unusually favourable occurrences on the field.

M m

maiden (maiden over) An over in which no runs are scored by the batsman. Additionally in one-day matches an over is considered a maiden only if no wides or no-balls were bowled.

maiden ball A term used humorously to mean a delivery on which no runs are scored off the bat.

maiden century The first score of one hundred or more runs by a batsman at the stated level of cricket.

make room (said of a batsman) To draw away from the line of the ball and create space to play a forceful shot on the off-side.

make the ground A run out or stumping chance saved by the batsman by his entering the popping crease just in time.

man of the match Formal recognition of the player who makes the most valuable contribution (batting, bowling and fielding combined) in a one-day match. The award – usually in the form of cash or a trophy/memento is presented immediately after the match.

man of the series Formal recognition – in the form of cash, or another award – of the player who records the most consistent performance during a test or one-day international series, taking into account batting, bowling, as well as fielding. The award is presented immediately after the conclusion of the series.

manager A person appointed to manage the administrative affairs of a team. His main functions include participation in selection i.e., the playing eleven, discussing/evolving team strategy, dealing with issues involving players, and dealing with public relations and other external matters.

mandatory overs The overs that a team must compulsorily bowl within the specified time, e.g. it is mandatory to bowl twenty overs in the last one hour of the final day of a test match.

Manhattan A computer generated bar chart used by television commentators in one-day matches to show the rate of scoring during an innings; so called because some of the bars for high-scoring overs appear like skyscrapers on the bar chart.

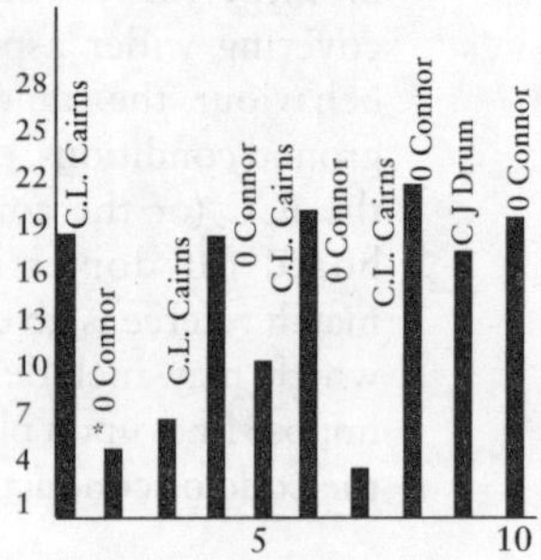

Manhattan graph

marking the stance The elaborate action of a batsman in taking guard and readying himself to face the bowling, particularly when he is new to the crease.

master blaster One of the frontline batsmen in the team who scores his runs very quickly, playing bold and attractive shots against all types of bowling. The term applies mainly to one-day cricket.

match abandoned Match called off during the scheduled time of play – sometimes with little or no play – due to bad weather or unplayable ground conditions.

match card An official card issued by some local cricket boards, listing the names of players (with photographs) authorised to represent a team. The umpires may verify the players against the match card before commencement of play.

match fees Fees paid to the players/teams for playing a match or to the umpires/officials for performing their duties in a match.

match-fixing Alleged involvement, or attempt thereof, in doctoring the match result for personal gain or to suit the bookmakers.

match referee An official appointed to monitor the conduct of the game, covering wider aspects like players' behaviour, the standard of umpiring, ground conditions, etc. Responsible to the ICC (or the country's governing board for domestic matches), the match referee is given varying powers which may include the authority to impose fines upon players for breaking the code of conduct.

matting A pitch-sized green carpet made of coir, used as the playing surface where a proper turf wicket is not available. It is laid on a well rolled strip of ground (pitch) and tightly pegged all around to avoid uneven bounce. A matting wicket has not been used in test matches since the early 1960s and its use in first-class matches is now very rare.

meat of the bat The central part of the bat, particularly around the lower half, which generates the maximum power when the ball is struck.

Mecca of cricket The Lord's ground in London. One of the oldest cricket grounds in the world, Lord's has the distinction of staging numerous historic cricket events, including four world cup finals. It is also the headquarters of the ICC and houses a unique cricket museum. See *Lord's*.

medium fast (medium pace) Denoting speed and a type of bowling which is quicker than spin bowling, but slower than true fast bowling. Medium pace bowlers typically bowl at a speed of between 60 to 70 miles an hour.

medium pacer A bowler who specialises in medium fast bowling. Medium pacers are normally brought in to attack after the fast bowlers have delivered a spell and can be used as attacking or defensive bowlers. The main strength of a medium pacer lies in his accuracy, variation of deliveries and ability to bowl longer spells.

mid-field Vast area of the field all around the wicket between close-in and deep positions. It includes all the standard field positions, like cover, mid-off, mid-on, square leg, etc.

mid-off A fielding position on the off-side, midway between the bowler and extra cover. The normal mid-off position is at a distance of 25 to 30 yards from the batsman. It is a relatively easier position to field as nearly all the shots come from straight-bat strokes. The main variations of mid-off are: **deep mid-off**, some 50 to 60 yards from the batsman; **short mid-off**, about 10 to 15 yards from the batsman; and silly **mid-off**, about 3 to 4 yards from the batsman.

mid-on A fielding position on the on-side, midway between the bowler and mid-wicket. It is normally the mirror image of mid-off, but can vary according to situation. The different placements along the mid-on line are: **deep mid-on**, some 50 to 60 yards from the batsman; **short mid-on**, about 10 to 15 yards from the batsman; and **silly mid-on**, about 3 to 4 yards from the batsman.

mid-wicket A fielding position on the on-side, midway between square leg and mid-on. The normal mid-wicket position is at a distance of 25 to 30 yards from the batsman and covers a relatively larger ground on either side of it. The main variations of this position are: **deep mid-wicket,** about 50 to 60 yards from the batsman; **short mid-wicket,** about 10 to 15 yards from the batsman; and **silly mid-wicket,** about 3 to 4 yards from the batsman.

mid-wicket conference A quick meeting on the pitch between the two playing batsmen to review the game strategy; normally held between overs when the field is changing.

middle *(1 batting)* To connect the ball with the central part of the bat; a sign of confident batting. *(2 ground)* Central part of the ground or pitch. Thus, 'in the middle' means batsmen at the wicket.

middle order A team's batting line-up between the openers and tail-enders. It consists of the foremost batsmen in the **early middle order** (numbers 3, 4 and 5), followed by the remaining recognised batsmen and all-rounders in the **late middle order** (numbers 6, 7 and sometimes 8). The middle order is expected to score the bulk of the team's total.

middle stance A stance in which the bat is held in line with the middle stump.

middle stump The central of the three wooden rods that comprise the wickets at either end of the pitch. An imaginary straight line drawn through the middle stumps and extended to the boundary line on either side divides the ground into two equal halves.

milking the bowling Said of a batsman who is batting comfortably and getting a regular flow of runs, without resorting to big hitting.

mini-series A short series lasting two to three weeks, involving no more than three tests and/or three one-day internationals.

mini world cup A short tournament in which at least the top six cricket nations participate, but the total number of matches played are far fewer than in the World Cup championship; e.g., the Benson & Hedges cup played in Australia in 1984. See also *ICC Knock-out.*

minor counties Refers to the smaller county teams in England which do not have first-class team status. At present there are twenty such minor county teams in England, split into two divisions (eastern and western) of ten each.

miscue A misconnected shot that goes high up in the air but does not travel far. Miscued shots often result in risky situations for the batsman, if not in actual dismissal through the catch taken.

misfield A failed attempt by the fielder at stopping the ball in play.

mishit A shot that does not connect properly with the bat and sends the ball in a direction different to that intended by the batsman.

miss A chance offered by the batsman (a catch or stumping) to dismiss him, but not taken by the fielding side.

miss out To fail to capitalise on an easy scoring opportunity—either a loose delivery, a weak spell of bowling or generally favourable batting conditions.

mistime A stroke lacking the precision of timing to be effective, resulting in the ball travelling uppishly, slowly or in a direction different to that intended by the batsman.

mix up Confusion between the two batsmen at the centre when attempting to take a run, resulting in a run out or the risk of it.

monopolise the innings An outstanding performance by a batsman who plays a long and responsible innings to score the majority of runs registered by his team.

monopolise the partnership Said of a batsman who scores a high percentage of the total runs scored in a partnership.

mop up the tail Said of a bowler or the bowling side, which captures the last few wickets of the batting team quickly and cheaply.

morning session The first session of play in a test or first-class match, from the start of play up to lunch, normally lasting two hours. In a one-day match played to standard day timings, the morning session may stretch up to three or more hours to allow for the batting side to complete its innings.

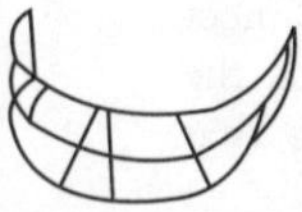

mouth guard

mouth guard A padded strap attached to the helmet and worn over the mouth for protection against the rising delivery of a fast bowler.

move *(1 bowling)* The ability of a bowler to make the ball deviate in the air or off the pitch; more applicable to fast, or medium fast bowling. *(2 captain)* A tactical change in batting, bowling or field placing done by the captain to get on top of the opposition in a particular situation during the match.

movement Deviation in a delivery, either in the air or off the pitch, achieved due to the skills of a bowler, or nature of pitch; applies mainly to fast or medium fast bowling.

mow Trimming of grass on the pitch before commencement of play, so that it does not unduly assist pace bowlers to the detriment of batsmen.

N n

neck The slightly angular construction of the bat where the handle connects with the blade.

neck and crop A complete miss by a batsman as he attempts to negotiate a delivery, usually by stretching forward, often resulting in a clean bowled dismissal with stumps knocked down.

negative bowling Employing dubious bowling tactics to slow down the pace of the game or deny the batsmen a fair opportunity to play strokes, like persistently bowling wide outside the off-stump.

Nelson An individual or team score of 111, or multiples thereof, considered a bogey, or unlucky.

nerves To play with application and coolness in a tight situation.

nervous nineties A situation where a batsman loses his momentum and becomes over-cautious when approaching a century.

net A U-shaped enclosure erected around the batting end of a practice pitch, made of cotton, or synthetic twine, knotted into a mesh. Its purpose is to prevent shots hit by the batsmen from travelling very far, or injuring players and spectators.

net run rate (NRR) A formula applied in one-day tournaments to determine the qualifying team for a higher round when this cannot be decided on the basis of match results alone. In simple terms, the NRR for a team is determined by the equation 'A-B' for all matches played up to that stage, where A = Runs Scored/Overs Faced, and B = Runs Conceded/Overs Bowled. The team with a better NRR has an advantage over the other teams with the same number of points in the qualifying matches.

nets Cricket practice or training in a net enclosure; also referred to as net practice.

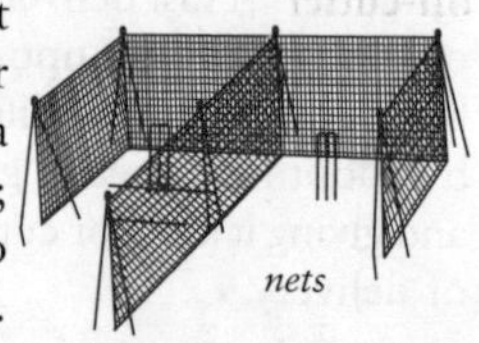
nets

neutral umpire An umpire who does not bear an affinity to any of the two contesting teams. For tests or one-day internationals, the neutral umpire is selected from the *ICC* panel of international umpires and belongs to a country other than the two playing countries.

new ball A new ball is taken at the beginning of an innings. In first-class matches, an additional new ball can be taken at the discretion of the fielding captain after at least 75 overs have been bowled with the old one.

new-ball bowler A fast bowler who opens the bowling.

new batsman A batsman who has come to the crease after the fall of a wicket and who hasn't yet settled down. Also referred to as new man in.

nick *(1)* A player's current form or effectiveness in batting or bowling. *(2)* A thin edged catch going to the wicket-keeper or the slip fielders.

night-cricket A cricket match or tournament played entirely under flood-lights.

nightwatchman A non-specialist batsman sent in to bat when a wicket falls towards the end of a day's play. This situation arises occasionally in the longer version of the game, and its intent is to protect a regular batsman who may be vulnerable in such conditions. The job of a nightwatchman is to at least survive until close of play.

nip A delivery that hastens after pitching due to the bowler's action and/or due to liveliness of the pitch.

no-ball An unfair delivery, commonly due to the bowler's foot overstepping the popping crease. The other no-ball situations are: *(i)* chucking, i.e. bowler straightening his arm at the time of delivery, *(ii)* bowler sending down an unduly hostile delivery, despite warning, and *(iii)* positioning of a fielder in a restricted area. A batsman is not given out to the bowler on a no-ball, and one extra run is added to the score as penalty. The bowler must also bowl an extra delivery to compensate for the no-ball.

umpire's signal for no-ball

no man's land Vacant area between two fielders or area of the field not covered by any fielder.

no result A match which does not end in any of the three possible results, viz. win/lose, draw or tie. Such rare occurrences result when a match is abandoned midway due to bad weather, or other interruptions.

no run A delivery on which no runs are scored. See *dot ball.*

non-striker One of the two batsmen at the wicket who is not facing the bowling; the batsman who stays at the far end of the wicket when the bowler is delivering a ball.

not cricket Cricket, said to be a gentleman's game, is expected to be played in a fair and sporting manner. Hence, 'its not cricket' means unfair play or something which is generally against the spirit of the game.

not out *(1)* An innings in which a batsman is not dismissed. A not out innings is denoted by an asterisk against the batsman's score in the scoresheet or when reporting abridged scores. *(2)* An appeal for dismissal not upheld by the umpire.

nudge A gentle push to deflect the ball in the area behind square, on either side of the wicket. The stroke relies on deft timing and placement to help the ball roll along on its own momentum.

O o

obstructing the field An unusual form of dismissal in which the batsman is declared out by the umpire for preventing or disturbing the fielders from taking a catch, or attempting a run out. In practice, such dismissals never happen and the provision exists under the laws only as a deterrent.

obstruction *(1)* Interference, or interception between the batsmen and fielders. The umpires are required to consider whether such instances were deliberate and take appropriate decisions. *(2)* Distractions caused to the players by external factors, like a batsman being obstructed by someone moving in front of the sight-screen when he is ready to face a delivery.

occupy the crease The length of batting time recorded by a batsman or a partnership, during an innings.

off The half side of the pitch and ground facing the batsman as he takes stance. See *off-side.*

off-break A delivery that turns after pitching from off- to leg-side of the wicket.

off-cutter A fast delivery moving from off-side to leg-side upon pitching. It is bowled by fast or medium fast bowlers by adopting a special grip on the ball and giving it a flip or cut at the moment of delivery.

off-drive A drive played to a ball pitching or coming up around the line of the off-stump, hitting it to the mid-off area. One of the safest strokes, it is played either off the front or back foot with a straight, full-flowing bat.

off-drive

off-side The entire one half of the field facing the batsman, comprising mid-off, cover, extra cover, point and third man areas. The off-side is separated from the on-side by an imaginary line passing vertically and centrally through the central stumps.

off-side field *(1)* Positioning of fielders on the off-side of the wicket. *(2)* A common field setting with fielders predominantly placed on the off-side, leaving fewer on the on-side.

off-side player A batsman who shows a higher propensity to play strokes on the off-side, as compared to the on-side; one who scores most of his runs through off-drives, cover drives, cuts and glides.

off-spin The technique of bowling spinning off-breaks or deliveries that turn after pitching from off-side to leg-side. The term typically refers to right-arm off-spin bowling, as faced by a right-hand batsman.

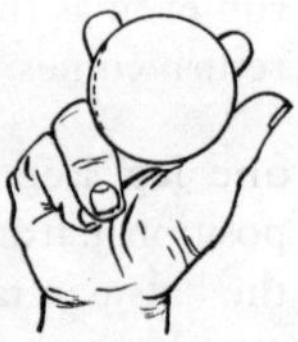

off-spin

off-spinner A bowler who sends down off-spin or off-break deliveries.

off-stance A stance where the bat is held in line with the off-stump. This stance is seldom used due to the high probability of getting out lbw.

off-stump The first of the three wooden rods that comprise the wickets, as viewed from the off-side. See *stumps*.

off the hips An improvised turn or flick shot played by the batsman to a rising delivery. The shot often proves productive by affording good placement over a wide area between mid-wicket and fine leg.

off the mark (said of a batsman, or team) To score the first runs or open account, after going into bat.

off the seam A fast or medium paced delivery that lands on the seam of the ball and deviates towards or away from the batsman.

off the toes A wristy shot played on the on-side, connecting the bat to the ball at toe level and turning, or flicking it over a wide area between mid-wicket and fine leg. Played mainly in forward motion, the shot relies on quick footwork and crisp timing to be most effective.

off the toes

off theory A strategy to dismiss or contain a batsman by bowling deliveries on or outside the off-stump with a packed off-side field. It is a common strategy in modern cricket, particularly when fast and medium fast bowlers are operating.

official scorer A person nominated by a team to record the detailed, ball by ball score of the match. For every match there are two such scorers (one from each team) who maintain separate scorebooks.

offie (offy) A right-arm off-spin bowler.

old ball A ball that has been used for several overs and has lost its shine and glaze. The characteristics of an old ball are that it is less responsive to swing bowling, but provides a better grip and turn for spin bowlers.

on The one half of the pitch and ground on which the batsman is standing as he faces a delivery. See *on-side.*

on a hat-trick A situation where a bowler has taken two wickets with two successive deliveries and is preparing to bowl the third delivery which could give him a hat-trick if a wicket is taken.

on-drive A drive played to a ball pitching or coming up around the middle and leg stump, hitting it to

on-drive

the mid-on area. One of the basic strokes, it is played with a straight and full flowing bat, but is not as popular with batsmen, as are other strokes.

on-side The entire one half of the ground and pitch behind the batsman, comprising mid-on, mid-wicket, square-leg and fine-leg areas. The on-side is separated from the off-side by an imaginary line passing vertically and centrally through the central stumps.

on-side field *(1)* Positioning of fielders on the on-side of the wicket. *(2)* A not very common type of field setting with fielders predominantly placed on the on-side, leaving fewer on the off-side.

on-side player A batsman whose ability and preference for strokes on the on-side is higher than those for the off-side; one who scores most of his runs through strokes like on-drives, sweeps, pulls, turns and flicks.

on the rise Playing the ball as it comes up near the body, as opposed to stretching forward or moving back to play it. A typical shot played on the rise is a forceful push or a drive, played with a full flow of the bat.

on the roll Batsman, bowler or the entire team, in full form and recording impressive performances.

one-day A match which is scheduled to be completed within a day, with both teams playing only one innings each of the stipulated number of overs and following the special rules of one-day cricket. A one-day match is noted for its fast and result oriented action. It contrasts with the longer version of the game (lasting three or more days) which is relatively slower, yet often resulting in a draw.

one-day international A one-day match between two national sides who are both members of the ICC.

one down Batting position, or the batsman who goes into bat, at the fall of the first wicket. Also referred to as no. 3 batting position or one drop.

one drop See *one down.*

one for the throw Said of a batsman who starts and completes an additional run even as the ball is fielded and the return comes in from the outfield.

one leg Leg guard, i.e. a marked position in front of the leg stump where the batsman takes stance. See also *leg guard.*

one-run-saving A field position or placement of fielders, aimed at preventing batsmen from taking singles.

one short A signal by the umpire to indicate that a batsman failed to reach inside the popping crease when taking two, or more, runs. The signal is given by touching the shoulder with the fingers, as the arm is raised horizontally. A short run is not counted, but the batsmen retain their respective ends.

umpire's signal for one short

open *(1)* To go out to bat at the beginning of an innings as one of the two batsmen (openers) to face the new ball. *(2)* To operate with a new ball as one of the first two bowlers at the start of an innings.

open account (said of a batsman or team) The first runs scored by a new batsman or the first runs scored for the team.

open chest action An unusual style of bowling in which the bowler's body and chest faces the batsman as the ball is delivered. This contrasts with the normal bowling action in which the body is pivoted sideways.

open-eyed stance See *two-eyed stance.*

open field Area of the field not covered by any of the fielders.

open the arms Said of a batsman who begins to attack the bowling with bold strokes, after a relatively slow or moderate start.

open the face of the bat A straight-bat shot, played by turning the face of the bat away from the body, in the direction of cover or point, in order to place the ball in the desired off-side area.

opener One of the two batsmen who start the innings for the batting team. The ability to play fast bowling skilfully, when the ball is new, is the main quality of an opener. For one-day matches, an ability to score runs quickly during the first fifteen overs is equally important.

opening batsman One of the two batsmen who start the innings for the batting team. See *opener.*

opening bowler One of the two fast, or medium fast bowlers who start the bowling attack with a new ball.

opening pair The two batsmen who commence batting or the two fast bowlers who commence bowling, at the start of an innings.

opening stand The partnership recorded by the first two batsmen at the start of an innings.

opening wicket First wicket or the opening partnership.

orthodox Conventional or copybook style in batting or bowling; a player in the conventional mould, e.g. orthodox left-arm spin bowler, orthodox opening batsman.

orthodox batting A conventional style of batting, executing the majority of the strokes with a straight bat and positioning the feet and body in perfect copybook style. It also involves selecting the right kind of strokes for a particular kind of delivery.

out Signifies the end of a batsman's innings; a dismissal. As per the Laws of Cricket, a batsman can be out in nine different ways: bowled, caught, lbw, stumped, run out, hit wicket, handled the ball, obstructing the field and timed out. The last three types of dismissals are, however, purely technical and seldom occur during matches.

umpire's signal to indicate batsman is out

outcricket The performance of a team in the fielding and catching departments, as distinct from batting, or bowling.

outfield Deep field or the part of the field which is closer to the boundary. Thus, an outfielder is a fielder positioned in the outfield.

outgoing delivery A delivery moving away from the batsman to outside the off-stump, either in the air or off the pitch.

outing A period of the game with players engaged in batting, bowling or fielding; may also refer to a session, a day, an inning, or a match.

outright Refers to a clear win/lose result achieved in the longer version of the game, with the losing team necessarily being all out in its second innings. The winning team, thus achieves an outright victory, while the losing team is said to suffer an outright loss.

outside Area of the crease or pitch, on either side of the stumps, i.e. outside off-stump or outside leg stump.

outside edge *(1)* A misconnected stroke, with the ball deflecting off the outer corner of the bat to the off-side area behind the wickets. *(2)* Outer corner of the bat pointing towards the off-side.

outswing A fast bowler's delivery that moves in the air from the on-side to the off-side. See also *away-swing.*

over *(1)* A spell of six consecutive deliveries sent down by a bowler. It is bowled from one end of the pitch, on completion of which the next over is bowled by another bowler from the other end. No-balls and wides are not counted as valid deliveries and are required to be rebowled in the same over. *(2)* A call made by an umpire to indicate the completion of an over. The umpire also signals by extending the hand and four finger in front of him to indicate the end of an over.

over-rate Refers to the average time taken to bowl an over or the number of overs sent down per hour. The average over-rate depends largely upon the type of bowlers in operation (fast, or slow) and the rate of scoring by the batsmen.

over-run To continue running beyond the batting crease after completing a run.

over-swing Imparting more swing than is necessary, thus deviating the ball wide from the stumps and rendering it ineffective.

over the top An aggressive shot, hitting the ball in the deep, over the heads of the close-in or mid-field fielders.

over the top

over the wicket A bowling action in which the ball is delivered with the bowling arm closer to the stumps. This contrasts with the round the wicket action, which is the alternate way of bowling.

overarm The standard form of bowling in which the arm is rolled forward and ball delivered from an over-head position. Invented by a woman, overarm bowling is now the only recognised form of bowling and contrasts with underarm bowling which is completely out of favour.

overbowl A situation in which a captain places excessive reliance on a bowler and gives him longer spells to bowl than seems justified.

overpitch A delivery pitched closer to the batsman, and relatively easier to play, typically producing a variety of front-foot drives.

overs per hour A measure of the speed at which the game is progressing in terms of overs bowled. Around 15 overs per hour is considered the average norm.

overstep (said of a bowler) To step beyond the popping crease while sending down a delivery; the most common reason for a no-ball being declared.

overthrow A return by a fielder that travels past the wickets, due to deflection a throw in the wrong direction or failure on the part of the other fielders to stop it. Additional runs taken as a result of the overthrow are simply added to runs originally scored.

P p

pace *(1)* Refers to the speed of bowling, like fast, medium fast or slow. *(2)* Also refers to the nature of the pitch, e.g. slow paced or fast paced.

pace bowling Refers to any of the three types of fast bowling, namely: genuine fast, fast medium or medium fast. At the international level, a bowling speed of 80 mph and above is considered genuine fast; between 70 and 80 mph, fast medium; and between 60 and 70 mph, medium fast.

paceman A bowler who bowls at a medium fast or higher speed.

pack To have a greater concentration of fielders in a particular area of the field in order to contain run scoring or pursue a plan to dismiss the batsman, e.g. to pack the off-side field.

Packer circus Refers to the series of one-day international matches privately organised by the Australian business tycoon, Kerry Packer, between 1979 and 1981. These matches were played between privately assembled 'national' teams, represented by rebel cricketers from those respective countries. The series was termed a 'circus' because many non-traditional concepts were introduced into the games, (like, day–night matches and coloured clothing) and the participating teams did not have any official recognition.

pad and bat An unintentional, faulty stroke in which the ball touches the bat after it has first hit the pad. The batsman can be declared out lbw or caught to such a delivery, as applicable.

pad away The action of a batsman in thrusting the pad forward and sideways to fend off or deflect a delivery.

pad play The repeated use of a pad, rather than the bat, by a batsman to fend off or deflect deliveries.

pad up (said of a batsman) *(1)* To put on pads in readiness for batting. *(2)* To take the front leg forward and across to deflect a delivery or to provide a safety barrier in case it deviates unexpectedly towards the stumps.

padding An obsolete term for pads or pad up.

paddle A kind of sweep shot played to a delivery pitching outside the leg stump, hitting the ball towards fine leg. So called because the shot resembles a paddle movement, with the bat moving vertically on the side of the batsman.

pads Protective gear worn on the legs by batsmen and wicket-keepers to avoid injury from the ball. They cover the legs from ankle up to lower thigh and are strapped behind to keep them firmly in place. Also referred to as leg guard.

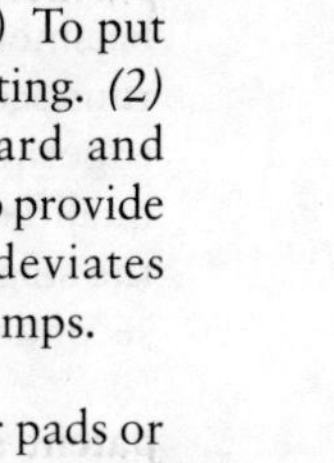

pads

pair A batsman out for a duck in both innings of a match.

pajama game A match, or tournament which does not represent serious competition and is played mainly for fun. A set of ad hoc rules may be followed in such games to make them more action-packed.

palm break Spin imparted on a delivery by rolling the palm over the ball. It is an alternate technique to turn the ball, as distinct from finger or wrist spin.

partner Refers to a batting or bowling partner; for example, when two batsmen are at the crease, each is a partner to the other; when two bowlers operate in tandem, each is a bowling partner to the other.

partnership The association of two batsmen at the wicket, measured by runs scored from the time they come together. A partnership is further qualified by a 'wicket prefix' denoting the stage at which it took place, e.g. a second wicket partnership.

patent shot The favourite shot of a batsman, executed with a touch of authority and individuality.

pavilion The main building usually at one end of the cricket ground, providing comfortable seating and a very good viewing angle. Intended primarily for use by players, officials, club members and guests, it also houses the administrative areas and amenities for the ground.

pavilion end Refers to the side of the ground or wickets, closer to the pavilion.

peaking Said of a player or team showing consistently improving performances in the matches before a major tournament or in its preliminary rounds, thus indicating that it will also perform well in the final matches.

peg An obsolete term for stump.

penalty *(1 team)* A monetary fine imposed upon a team guilty of a slow over-rate or infringement of rules. In one-day matches, the penalty may also result in a reduction in the number of overs allowed to the guilty team to achieve its target. *(2 player)* A monetary fine imposed on a player for unfair play or for breaking the game's code of conduct; e.g., a penalty may be imposed for protesting against or questioning the umpire's decision.

performance bonus An additional reward given to players or teams over and above the contracted amount, for achieving the specified results.

physical trainer A person qualified to administer programmed physical training to the players to improve their physical fitness. He is usually employed by a team on an ad hoc basis for coaching/conditioning camps before the start of a season, series or tournament.

pick The ability of a batsman to spot or read, the characteristics of a delivery – speed, line, length, swing, etc. – before playing it. The two variations of this term are: to **pick early,** to spot the type of delivery at an early stage and either play, or leave it with comfort; to **pick late,** to spot the type of delivery at a very late stage and play it hurriedly or fail to play it competently.

pick the gap To score runs by placing the ball in a vacant area or between two fielders.

pick-up A fielder's action of picking up the ball from the ground, especially when performed skilfully while running.

pick-up and throw The smooth, flowing action of a fielder in picking up the ball from the ground and returning it to the batting or bowling end, to contain run scoring or to attempt to run out the batsman. It is a basic element of efficient ground fielding.

picking the fielder A batsman deliberately playing the ball to a weak fielder for easier run scoring.

pinch-hitter A batsman sent in to play attacking shots and score quick runs by taking advantage of the field restrictions during the first fifteen overs of the innings in a one-day match. A pinch-hitter's role is ideally played by an all-rounder, reputed for bold hitting.

pinned down(said of a batsman) To be unable to score runs for a long time due to accurate bowling and sharp fielding.

pitch*(1)* The strip at the centre of the ground on which batting and bowling is performed. It measures 66 feet in length and 10 feet in width (between the two sets of stumps) and can be made of natural turf or artificial material. Also called wicket. *(2)* The spot where the bowler's delivery lands. The variations of this term are: **pitch short,** to pitch short of good length; **pitch-up,** to pitch closer to the batsman; **overpitch,** to pitch within easy reach of the batsman.

pitch cover A canvas, or polyethylene sheet laid on the pitch to prevent damage from rain or bad weather.

pitch invasion Interruption in play due to spectators running on to the pitch to congratulate a player—mainly a batsman, for achieving a batting landmark. See also *crowd invasion.*

place (placement) A deliberate stroke by a batsman to put the ball in an intended area to score runs; e.g., to place the ball between point and cover.

play The term has several meanings depending upon context, viz. *(1)* the proceedings of the game or a match in action; *(2)* the performance of a team; *(3)* the schedule of matches; *(4)* the skill or ability of a batsman to negotiate the bowling. *(5)* Also a technical term used by the umpire to announce the commencement or resumption of the game after a longish break.

play across To play cross bat. See also *across the line.*

play against the spin To play a stroke in the direction opposite to the spin of the ball; normally refers to a situation in which the batsman quickly spots the nuances of the delivery and goes for a forcing shot or placement.

play and miss A failed attempt by a batsman to play a stroke, especially when playing deliveries outside the off-stump.

play back(said of a batsman) To play a straight-bat stroke going on the back foot, with the body positioned well inside the batting crease. The advantage of playing back is that it allows the batsman a fraction of a second longer to watch the delivery and play the intended stroke.

play forward (said of a batsman) To play a stroke by going on the front foot and meeting the ball several feet in front of the batting crease. The advantage of playing forward is that it allows the batsman to execute a stroke based on the trajectory of the delivery, thereby avoiding having to negotiate its bounce and turn after pitching.

play out(said of a batsman) To play a delivery in a cautious, defensive manner in front of the wickets.

play out the time Batting with the main aim of completing the available time remaining or the overs, rather than to score runs.

play over Said of a batsman who swings the bat above the ball, due to wrong judgement of the height or bounce, thus failing to make any contact.

play with the head down To bat in a correct and controlled manner.

play with the spin To play a stroke by angling or turning the bat in the direction of the spin, thus using the natural momentum of the ball to good effect.

played on A kind of dismissal in which the ball is deflected or rolls on from the bat, to hit the stumps and dislodge the bails. The dismissal is recorded as bowled in the scoresheets and the wicket is credited to the bowler.

player A member of the team, including the reserves. In general terms it also refers to anyone who plays the game regularly.

Players Refers to the classification of professional cricketers, as distinct from amateurs (or Gentlemen), that existed in England until 1962. The Players received a professional fee for playing matches, while the Gentlemen played as a hobby. There was often a healthy rivalry between the two, the high point of which was the annual Gentlemen versus Players match. These classifications were abolished in 1962.

players' room A room in the pavilion reserved for the teams (normally one for each team) playing the match, in which players can rest and change.

Playfair Cricket A famous monthly and annual cricket publication from England. While specialising in the coverage of English cricket, it also covers international cricket matches and cricketing stories.

playing for record Situation in a match when a batting record for an individual, or team is within sight, and the game is focused on equalling or breaking the record, rather than playing for a quick result.

playing for time Situation in a match where batsmen are content to stay at the wicket, either to prolong the innings and avert defeat or simply wait for batting conditions to improve; less relevant for one-day matches, this is not uncommon in first-class cricket.

playing with the head up An incorrectly executed batting stroke, appearing clumsy and risking dismissal.

plod To bat laboriously, finding it difficult to play the bowling or score runs confidently; A **plodder** is a batsman who bats laboriously.

pluck To take a flying catch at a close-in position, more by reflex action than judgement.

plucky knock To show character and courage in staying at the wicket and scoring runs when wickets are falling at the other end against an effective bowling and fielding attack.

plumb Clearly out; refers mainly to lbw situations, with the ball striking the pads right in front of the wickets.

plumb in front (plumb leg before) Unquestionably out lbw, with the ball following the plumb line (perpendicular) to the stumps.

plunder To score runs heavily, taking advantage of weak bowling or easy batting conditions.

point A fielding position square on the off-side, some 20 to 25 yards from the wicket, more or less in line with the popping crease. It is one of the busiest positions on the field, with balls coming frequently both from defensive strokes as well as from well-timed cuts and pushes.

poor cricket A general expression, meaning lower standards displayed in any aspect of the game, e.g. bad selection of shots (batting), unimaginative field settings (captaincy), dropped catches (fielding), under- or over-pitched deliveries (bowling), etc.

poor light Conditions where the ground light is inadequate for the batsman to see the ball clearly.

poor start Refers to either of two situations in a match: *(1)* batting side losing early wickets or struggling for runs and falling behind on the scoring rate; *(2)* bowling side giving away runs through wayward bowling and/or missed opportunities for dismissal.

pop-up *(1 bowling)* A delivery that rises steeply and unexpectedly after pitching, due to imperfections in the wicket. *(2 batting)* To play the ball up in the air for an easy close-in catch.

popping crease A horizontal line drawn on the pitch, parallel to the bowling crease, at a distance of four feet in front of the stumps. The area behind the popping crease marks the batsman's territory. Also referred to as batting crease.

position *(1 fielding)* The name of a spot or area on the field in relation to the batsman, e.g. slip, point or gully. *(2 fielding)* To place a fielder at a particular spot or area on the field. *(3 batting)* The batting order in which a batsman is slotted to bat (e.g. one down).

post To score a good number of runs as an individual batsman, in partnership, or for the team total.

practice cage Practice pitch surrounded by a strong net to prevent the ball from travelling far or injuring the players.

practice pitch An additional pitch provided in the corner of the ground for the players to practice on.

pressure tactics Tactical moves by the captain of the fielding side to put the batsman under pressure, expecting that he will commit errors and get out, e.g., by setting an attacking field for a new batsman at the crease.

prize money A nominated cash award for the team or players, for winning matches or achieving success in a tournament.

productive over An over in which many runs are added to the total, counting runs scored by the batsmen as well as those taken as extras.

professional cricketer A person whose main occupation is playing cricket, and who is paid an agreed fee for playing. Professional cricketers are more commonly found in England due to the prevalent system of contracting players to play one or two seasons for a club.

protection An area of the field which a fielder is able to move over and cover.

protector See *abdominal guard* or *box*.

pull A cross-batted shot, swinging the ball across the line, anywhere between mid-wicket

pull

and backward square leg. Mostly played off the back foot, the pull is popular as well as productive. The ideal delivery for a pull is one pitching short of length, on the middle, leg or outside the leg stump.

pull-drive An unorthodox stroke, combining the elements of a pull and an on-drive. The movement of the feet for this shot is similar to a pull, but the bat is swung more perpendicular than horizontal, hitting the ball to the mid-wicket area.

punch A ground shot played off the back foot, on either side of the wicket, hitting the ball with a quick and powerful flow of the bat, and connecting with it right in the middle.

punish Authoritative strokeplay and free scoring by the batsman or team, due to superior batting or due to a weak bowling attack.

push A stroke halfway between defending and driving. Played with a straight bat, the push is ideally employed for scoring ones and twos by placing the ball safely.

push through *(1)* A spinner's delivery bowled at a flatter and quicker pace than his normal deliveries. *(2)* Bowling the over or a spell, hurriedly, with the primary aim of saving time rather than taking wickets; applicable in situations when the bowling sides have to catch up with a lagging over-rate.

put down (said of a fielder) To drop a catch or a possible catch.

put in A situation where the captain winning the toss asks the opposing team to bat first.

put into bat A team asked to bat first by the opposing captain despite losing the toss.

put on A batting partnership qualified by runs added by the pair of batsmen.

PWC rating A system of rating the players and teams based on their current performance in international matches. The ratings are named after the renowned auditing firm, Price-Waterhouse-Coopers (PWC), which administers and publishes the ratings.

Q q

quick run A well judged, sharp single taken by placing the ball close to a fielder.

quick running Refers to good coordination and fast running between the wickets by the batsmen.

quicker one A flatter and faster delivery bowled by a spin bowler to surprise the batsman. A medium pacer may also bowl a faster than normal delivery, but it is less noticeable.

quickie A fast bowler or paceman.

quota The maximum number of overs a bowler can bowl in a one-day match, which is a fifth of the total number of overs in the innings.

R r

rabbit A tail-ender or lower order batsman who has few batting skills and so is not expected to last long at the wicket.

rain-affected Refers to the adverse effects of rain on the progress of a match. This includes loss of time, cloudy weather, damp wicket, soggy outfield and conditions generally unfavourable for batting.

raise the bat See *acknowledge.*

raise the finger Refers to the umpire's action of declaring a batsman out by raising his index finger, following an appeal by the fielding side.

rankings The system of placing all participating teams and players in comparative order, based on their performance over a specified period. The rankings are often commercially sponsored (e.g. Ceat Rankings) and calculated separately for the shorter and longer versions of the game.

read *(1 batting)* The ability of a batsman to judge a bowler's delivery-its line, length, flight, pace, etc., e.g. to read a googly and play it safely. *(2 captaincy)* The ability of the captain to judge the nature of a wicket in terms of bounce, turn, pace, etc., e.g. to read the fast pace of the wicket and ask the opposing team to bat first.

rear Ball rising suddenly from good length or short of the good length spot, due to extra bounce in the wicket or extra effort on the part of the bowler.

reckless shot An unwarranted attacking shot played by a batsman, particularly when the situation demands control and discretion.

record Cricket is a game of a myriad records, both for the team and the individual in batting, bowling, wicket-keeping and fielding. Records are further subclassified by season, period, grounds, opponents, level of competition etc. A record, thus refers to any such official entry, or reference.

record book A figurative term, referring to the collection or existence of certain cricket records. In reality, cricket records are so many, and so frequently changing, that maintaining a comprehensive and up to date record book requires patience, dedication and long-term following of the game.

red ball The normal red cricket ball used in all matches, as distinct from the white cricket ball used for day-night one-day matches.

red light Refers to the red light switched on by the third umpire to uphold an appeal for run out or stumping, after watching the television replays. This situation, however, is limited to international matches and those high level first-class matches where a third umpire and television replay facility are available.

reduced target A situation in a one-day match when, due to unscheduled loss of time, the victory target for the team batting second is reduced along with a reduction in the number of overs.

regulation slip catch A typical slip catch coming at a comfortable height from the outside edge of the bat.

replacement ball A ball is replaced during an innings with an equally old ball if it loses shape or is lost in play. In one-day matches (played with a white ball), a replacement ball may also be allowed if the original one becomes dirty.

reply The total registered by a side batting second against the target set by the side batting first.

reserve A player included in the overall team, but not in the playing eleven, nor as twelfthman. A reserve player is allowed to field (though not in specialist positions) when one of the regular fielders leaves the field due to injury or any other valid reason, but is not allowed to bowl or keep wickets.

reserve day An extra day (if any) set aside under tournament rules to make up for the time lost due to unexpected stoppage in play. This is done to secure a definite result instead of a draw.

rest day *(1)* A day earmarked for the players to rest in a five-day test or first-class match. A standard feature up to the seventies, a rest day is rarely allowed now in order to save costs. *(2)* A day on which there are no matches, in an otherwise busy tournament.

result wicket A pitch for a test or first-class match that assists bowlers and helps achieve a win/lose result. It contrasts with batting wickets where teams amass big totals and the matches often end in a draw.

resumption of play Continuation of the match after a long rest, e.g., resumption after lunch or tea break or on the following day.

retire Said of a player who decides to stop playing competitive cricket at the given level (test, first-class or club).

retired hurt Inability of a batsman to continue batting due to injury sustained during the innings. The incomplete innings is considered not out in the computation of batting averages and is recorded 'retired hurt' in the scoresheet.

retired out Situation where a batsman discontinues his innings without being dismissed. Although very rare, this may be done to give another batsman a chance to come to the crease.

retrieve A part of the fielding skill to chase, stop and return a ball that is struck well past the fielder. This necessarily includes the ability to send in a quick and accurate throw back to the bowler or wicket-keeper.

return *(1 fielding)* Throw sent in by a fielder after stopping the ball. *(2 bowling)* The bowling performance recorded by a bowler during a match.

return catch A catch offered to or taken by the bowler; a caught-and-bowled dismissal.

return

return crease The straight line drawn perpendicular to the popping crease, extending four feet behind the stumps on both sides. The distance from the nearest stump to the return crease is also four feet. A bowler's feet must be within the return crease at the time of delivery, failing which the delivery will be declared a no-ball.

reverse sweep An unconventional and hazardous sweep shot, hitting the ball on the off-side, anywhere between backward point and third man. As with the sweep shot, the batsman goes down on one knee and hits the ball with a horizontal and downward swing of the bat, except that the actions are reversed from leg-side to off-side. The reverse sweep is typically played against spinners to exploit fielding gaps, particularly when quick runs are needed.

reverse sweep

reverse swing A variation of swing bowling in which the ball moves in the air in the opposite direction to what one would expect judging from the bowler's action. The reverse swing delivery is a relatively recent addition to a fast bowler's armoury. It is bowled with an older ball, making use of the difference in shine on its two halves, and requires immense ball control to deliver effectively.

revised target See *reduced target.*

right-arm A bowler who bowls with his right-arm. This is the most common form of bowling and has many variations, like right-arm fast or medium fast, right-arm leg-spin, right-arm off-spin, etc.

right-left combination *(1 batting)* A partnership involving one right-hand and one left-hand batsman. This is often a problem for the fielding side, as it requires field settings to be changed constantly, and bowlers to vary their length and direction of balls depending on which batsman they are bowling to. *(2 bowling)* A bowling attack with a left-arm bowler operating from one end and a right-arm bowler from the other. This gives the batsman an increased variety of bowling to face as the left- and right-hand bowlers would send down considerably different types of deliveries.

ring Fielders placed in catching or one-run-saving positions around the batsman, so as to form a ring or circle.

rising delivery A fast bowler's delivery that gains disconcerting height, making it difficult for the batsman to negotiate.

roller Solid, metallic equipment used to firm, level and recondition the pitch. Once a match is in progress, a roller can only be used before start of the day's play or in the recess between two innings. The batting side may decide which of the two rollers to use—the heavy or the light roller.

roller

rope A rope is used to mark the playing circumference of the field within the ground. Hence the term is synonymous with fence or boundary.

rotating strike Batsmen at the wicket taking singles regularly to keep the scoreboard moving, as well as to unsettle the bowling/fielding plans with frequent changes of strike. This is particularly effective when one right-handed and one left-handed batsmen are at the crease.

rough (rough patch) A small area on the side of the popping crease that sometimes gets effected by the bowler's foot marks. In the later stages of a match, a spinner's delivery pitched in this area is likely to take increased turn or behave abnormally.

round-arm An unusual bowling action in which the bowling arm is rolled and ball delivered slightly above shoulder height, but well below the normal over-head delivery position. A full round-arm action is seldom seen in modern-day cricket.

round robin A tournament, or part thereof, in which every team plays every other team and points are awarded based upon results. The teams achieving the highest tally of points then qualify to play the next or final round of matches.

round the wicket One of the two styles of bowling, in which the bowling arm is away from the wickets as the ball is delivered. It enables the bowler to bowl with a different angle and try new ways to dismiss or contain the batsman. See *over the wicket*.

rubbing or shining the ball

rub the ball on the trousers Refers to the action of a bowler in giving the ball a shine by rubbing it on the trousers. Fast bowlers do this habitually in order to improve the shine and get a higher movement of the delivery in the air.

rubber A test, or one-day international series, involving three or more matches.

ruled out An appeal for dismissal upheld by the umpire under doubtful, or debatable circumstances. It involves mainly lbws or close catches (including caught behind) dismissals.

run The basic unit of scoring off a single delivery. A run is scored when the two batsmen at the wicket run from their respective ends and safely reach the opposite ends. A maximum of six runs may be scored off a single delivery. Runs coming off the bat are credited to the batsman's score, and those not scored off the bat are counted as extras. The aggregate of all the runs scored by a team makes up its total.

run a ball A measure of scoring rate equating to six runs per over. It is considered a brisk rate of scoring, in all forms of cricket, particularly when maintained over a long period.

run a minute A measure of the scoring rate, equating to sixty runs per hour. Considered a fairly fast scoring rate for test and first-class matches, it is less relevant in one-day matches, where the rate of runs per over is more important.

run chase A riveting situation in which a team batting second seeks to achieve a challenging target with quick scoring.

run out A mode of dismissal in which the fielding side strikes the wicket (or dislodges the bails) with the ball, with the batsman out of his ground (i.e. when he fails to reach inside the popping crease). The dismissal is not credited to the bowler, but is recorded as 'run out' in the scoresheet. Runs scored off the delivery prior to the run out remain valid.

run rate The average number of runs scored by a team against the stated measure, mainly 'runs per over' in one-day matches and 'runs per hour' in tests or first-class matches. The average is either for the whole innings, or a part thereof, as stated.

run saving A defensive field setting primarily intended to prevent the batsman from scoring runs rather than to dismiss him with concentrated effort. Fielders in run-saving positions are, thus, mostly placed in the outfield or closer to the boundary positions.

run the ball down To play the ball with a straight but angled bat, so as to allow the ball to roll on its own force in the area between backward point and fine third man.

run through (said of a bowler or the bowling side) To send down highly effective bowling and capture a number of wickets or dismiss the entire team, for a modest total.

run-up The running or ambling movement of a bowler from the top of his bowling mark until delivery. The length and manner of running depends upon the bowler's individual style and comfort; it can be as little as a couple of steps for spinners, to as long as 15 to 20 yards for fast bowlers.

run-up

runner An alternate team member who does the running on behalf of an injured batsman. This is allowed only if the batsman is injured during the match. The runner is usually one of the dismissed batsmen and must wear all the equipment which the batsman wears, like pads, gloves, helmet, etc.

running between the wickets Refers to the skills required of a batsman in taking runs, i.e. good judgement, quick calling, fast running and coordination with the partner.

running catch A catch taken in the deep by running some distance towards a dropping ball. The agility, anticipation and precision of the fielder in taking a running catch is often spectacular to watch.

runs drying up An expression used to describe a gradual decline in the scoring rate due to the dominance of the bowlers and fielders.

runs per hour A measure of the scoring rate in an innings, indicating the average number of runs scored per hour by the batting side. This measure is used mainly in the longer version of the game and does not have as much relevance in one-day matches.

runs per over *(1)* A measure of the scoring rate, indicating the average number of runs scored or required to be scored, per over by the batting side. *(2)* A performance measure for a bowler, indicating the average number of runs conceded per over.

S s

safe pair of hands A reliable fielder who seldom misfields or drops catches.

safe total A team score considered unlikely to be overtaken by the opposition, thus making victory a strong possibility.

save *(1 fielding)* To perform tidy fielding and prevent runs. *(2 batting team)* To put up a fighting batting performance in adverse circumstances, and score enough runs to prevent defeat or post a decent total.

save the follow-on (said of a team) To achieve at least the minimum total required in the first innings to avoid being asked to follow on by the opposing team.

scalp A wicket taken by a bowler.

schedule A programme of matches to be played by teams during a stated period, e.g., a tour schedule or a tournament schedule.

score *(1)* The number of runs made by a team at a particular point in an innings, suffixed or prefixed by the number of wickets lost, e.g. 200 for five (or five for 200, as in Australia and New Zealand). If all the wickets have fallen in an innings, then the team score is simply stated by the number of runs made, with or without adding the words all out. *(2)* The number of runs made by an individual batsman at a particular point in an innings.

score box A wooden cabin reserved for the exclusive use of the scorers and placed at a vantage point on the periphery of the ground. The front of the box doubles up as a scoreboard, while the space inside is used to store the equipment used to display the scores.

scoreboard A large board placed or erected at the ground to display match scores and individual batting and

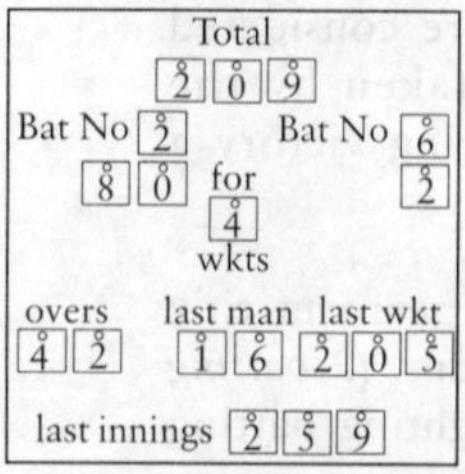

scoreboard

bowling performances of the players during the match.

scorebook A bound book containing many scoresheets. Each team maintains its own scorebook, which also makes for a permanent and detailed record of all the matches played by the team during a season or tournament.

scorecard A summarised scoresheet, giving the team scores with individual batting and bowling performances in a standard format. It is commonly used for reporting the match result to the press, as well as to the governing body under whose organisation the match is played.

scorer A person appointed by the team (normally one from each side) to do the scoring. He is required to follow the umpire's signals and concentrate on every single ball and do the scoring. This is a specialist function.

scoresheet A formatted sheet of paper used to record the ball by ball progress of a match. One scoresheet is used per innings, to record all the details for batting, bowling and run-scoring of the particular innings. A number of scoresheets together form a scorebook. See also *scorer* and *scoring*.

scoring *(1)* The specialist job carried out by the scorer of recording, on a scoresheet, the ball by ball progress of a match. It includes responding to the umpire's signals and continually cross checking to ensure accuracy. *(2)* The action of batting and accumulating runs by an individual batsman or the team.

scoring rate The speed at which runs are scored in comparison with the number of balls or overs faced, or minutes/hours consumed, in batting. The common measure of a scoring rate is runs per over in one-day matches and runs per hour in first-class matches.

scoring shot A stroke played by a batsman that results in a run or runs being scored.

seam The prominent stitches around the circumference of the ball which join the two halves of the leather casing around it. Skilled bowlers (particularly seamers) are able to work on the seam of the ball to get movement off the pitch.

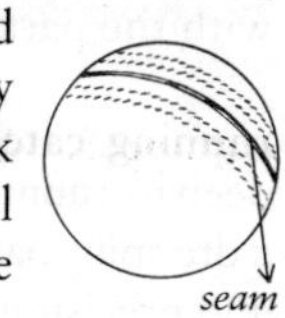

seam bowling A kind of fast or medium fast bowling in which the bowler tries to get the ball to deviate off the wicket by pitching it on the seam. Certain type of wickets, particularly in cold countries, are conducive to seam bowling.

seam-up A style of medium pace bowling in which the seam is kept straight facing the batsman, as the bowler delivers the ball. It is bowled with the expectation that the ball will deviate either way or kick up, if it lands on the seam.

seamer A bowler who specialises in the art of seam bowling.

season A period of the year, lasting anywhere between four to ten months, during which cricket is intensively played and all the important matches and tournaments in the country are conducted.

seasoned bat *(1)* A bat that has been properly oiled and stroked with an old ball to improve its performance.

See *seasoning*. *(2)* An experienced batsman who can be relied upon to bat steadily in a tight situation.

seasoned campaigner An experienced player – batsman or bowler – who has been through several testing situations and can be relied upon to pull the team out of trouble.

seasoning The curing of a new bat through the programmed application of linseed oil and careful knocking with an old ball to improve its performance.

second slip An off-side fielding position behind the batsman and between the first and third slips. It is mainly deployed when a fast bowler is operating with a new ball.

selection camp A gathering of potential players at the nets to display their skills and fitness to selectors. Such camps are particularly useful at the junior level where the selection is often made from a large number of less known players.

selector One of several persons appointed by the state, national governing board or club management, to jointly select the team through the selection committee.

send back *(1)* Batsman or non-striker not interested in a run and asking the other to go back. *(2)* Dismissal of a batsman, particularly when it is done quickly or without his scoring many runs.

send down To bowl a delivery, over or a spell of bowling.

series An agreed number of test or one-day matches played as part of a single tour between a visiting team and the host team.

session A period of play before a long break. In a first-class match, there are three standard sessions on each day, viz., morning, afternoon and evening sessions. A one-day match has only two sessions – one for each team's batting – separated by a longish break.

set *(1 batting)* To become familiarised with the pace and bounce of the wicket and bat with confidence. *(2 team)* To leave a defined target of runs to be achieved by the opposing team.

set a field To arrange fielding or to place fielders in the desired positions.

set a trap A planned and coordinated manoeuvre by the captain, bowler and fielders to dismiss a batsman. It involves precise field placement and bowling to a plan, to entice the batsman to play strokes that would result in his dismissal.

set-up A trap laid to dismiss a batsman.

settling down *(1 batsman)* To get the eye in and start playing with confidence. *(2 bowler)* To get a feel for the line and length and start bowling effectively.

seven-a-side A shortened version of the game, played with seven players on each side. The length of each innings is restricted to a maximum of seven overs to complete the innings quickly. Several other ad hoc rules are also applied, e.g. each player on the fielding side must bowl one over, and a batsman must retire once his individual score crosses thirty runs. The matches are always played in an atmosphere of enjoyment as opposed to seriousness.

shape Movement by a batsman to execute a stroke, without actually playing it.

Sharjah A small port city in the United Arab Emirates, which holds the world record for hosting the maximum number of one-day international matches. The record is significant considering that cricket is not the national game in the United Arab Emirates, which is only an associate member of the ICC. The support and following for the game there comes entirely from the large cricket-crazy expatriate population. International cricket tournaments are held in Sharjah twice a year under the banner, 'Cricketer's Benefit Fund Series'.

sharp catch

sharp catch A fast catch taken close to the wicket, largely through reflex action.

sharp chance A difficult split second catch going to the wicket-keeper, the close-in fielders, or the bowler himself, which is not taken.

sharp single A risky run taken just in time, even as the fielder pounces on the ball and attempts to run the batsman out.

sheet anchor A batsman who holds the innings together, playing a patient and responsible knock.

shielding Attempt by a senior or more established batsman at the crease to dominate the strike as much as possible, so as not to expose the other weaker batsman to the bowling.

shine The glaze, or polish on a new ball which helps fast bowlers get swing and bounce. The shine wears off as the ball is used during play.

shock bowler A fast or freakish bowler used sparingly and brought in to bowl short spells to attack the batsmen, particularly when a new batsman is at the crease.

shooter A delivery that unexpectedly keeps very low and comes hurriedly after pitching on an imperfect spot. It is the delivery most dreaded by batsmen as it leaves them little time to play a proper shot.

short A prefix used to describe any fielding position which is closer to the batsman then the corresponding normal position. The short positions are primarily deployed for catching, but can also be used to pressurise the batsman. The common short positions are: short gully, short point, short leg, short mid-off, short mid-on, short mid-wicket and short-cover.

short boundary Refers to the distance between the wicket and the boundary line which is comparatively shorter than the other boundaries or when compared to an average-sized ground, e.g., due to the oval shape of the ground, the point and square boundaries are often shorter than the other boundary positions.

short cut A restrained cut shot played with a shorter swing of the bat and less power. It is mainly deployed to achieve a better placement of the ball, when the batsman is constrained from playing a full flowing stroke.

short pitch A bowler's delivery landing around the middle of the pitch. It is considered a bad delivery as the batsman gets enough time to play it safely (often a bold hit) or leave it alone.

short run *(1)* A run in which either of the two batsmen fails to reach ground

umpire's signal for short run

(i.e. enter the popping crease) before taking off for the subsequent run. The umpire signals a short run by raising his hand horizontally and touching the shoulder with his fingers. The short run is not counted but the batsmen retain their respective ends. See also one short. *(2)* A quick single taken by the batsman by placing the ball in a nearby vacant area.

short tour An overseas tour lasting 2 to 4 weeks, during which no more than three tests and three one-day internationals are played, with or without a couple of other matches on the side.

shortened game A one-day match in which the stipulated overs are reduced for one or both teams, due to time lost on account of bad weather or unsuitable ground conditions.

shortened run-up Instance of a pace bowler cutting down his regular run-up to complete the over quickly, concentrate on accuracy or simply to save energy.

shorter version of the game Refers to the limited-over (one-day) matches, as opposed to tests or first-class matches which are the longer versions of the game.

shot Ball played by a batsman, which is hit with power and timing in any direction and in any manner. The term more aptly describes the hits made in front of the wickets, rather than square or behind.

shoulder arms (shoulder up) The action of a batsman to leave a delivery alone after covering the wickets with his pads and raising the bat away from the ball; done when the batsman considers it safer to let the ball pass on to the wicket-keeper than to play it.

shoulder delivery A ball bowled with extra force coming from the shoulder, resulting in quicker pace or higher bounce.

shoulder up See *shoulder arms.*

shout A loud appeal to the umpire to declare the batsman out, following a tenable case for dismissal. This kind of appeal comes mostly from the bowler and is a mix of frustration and hope.

show match A match which is not a part of the main series or tournament, but played mainly for the purpose of bringing top level cricket to the chosen venue. It is typically played between a visiting team and a local/national selection.

shuffle across The quick movement of feet by a batsman towards the off-stump to get closer to the ball, in an attempt to play it or leave it alone.

sideways bowling action A bowling action in which the bowler's body is pivoted on one side at the time of delivery. This type of bowling action is more common as compared to the other, open-chested, bowling action.

sight The skill and sharpness with which a batsman is able to judge the delivery and play it confidently. It often takes a few overs for a new batsman at the wicket to get his sight properly settled.

sight-screen (or sight-board) A large frame fitted with canvas or hardboard placed outside the boundary line, directly in front of the batting wickets on either side of the ground to help the batsman sight the ball properly. The screen (or board) is painted white, except for day and night matches where it is black or dark blue to contrast against the white ball used. A normal sized sight-screen can be as much as 40 feet in width and 15 feet in height so that it serves the purpose for both over the wicket and round the wicket bowling.

signals Various motions made or actions performed, by umpires to govern play—like, raising the index finger up to declare the batsman out.

signing a bat At the commercial level, bats are signed by renowned cricketers to endorse their good quality and improve their sales. At other times, bats are signed by players and officials as mementos or simply for collectors of autographs.

silly A prefix used to describe a fielding position which is very close (just 3–4 yards) to the batsman, as compared to its normal position. These positions are deployed to take close-in catches, as well as to put pressure on the batsman. The main silly positions are silly mid-off, silly mid-on, silly point and silly mid-wicket.

silly run A very risky run taken – with, or without success – when the ball is close to a fielder and he has a clear opportunity to run the batsman out.

silly run out Poor judgement in taking a run, resulting in an easy run out.

single One run scored off a delivery, either from a stroke or as bye/leg-bye, with both batsmen crossing over from one side of the wicket to the other.

single saving A field position aimed at preventing the batsman from taking a single (as opposed to a catching or boundary-saving position).

single wicket cricket A variant of traditional cricket in which players are individually pitted against one another to determine the best performer. Each player takes his turn at bowling and batting, which are both restricted to the specified number of balls per innings. Fielding support is provided by the common fielders. Scoring is done in the normal way, but several ad hoc rules are applied to make the game short and entertaining. These games are quite uncommon and are usually organised as short, commercial tournaments to show some of the popular players in action.

sitter An easy catch.

six-a-side An unofficial, shortened version of the game, with each team using only six players. Several ad hoc rules are applied for these matches, for instance, each side is restricted to six overs per innings, each player bowls only one over per innings, two runs are awarded for wide, a no-ball, etc. The main purpose of such games is enjoyment by non-regular cricket enthusiasts, aiming to complete the whole match in about an hour.

six an over A convenient and alternate measure of scoring rate, equal to a run a ball.

six (sixer) A lofted shot sending the ball sailing over the entire length of the field, to fall on, or outside the boundary line. Six runs are awarded for such a shot, which is the maximum

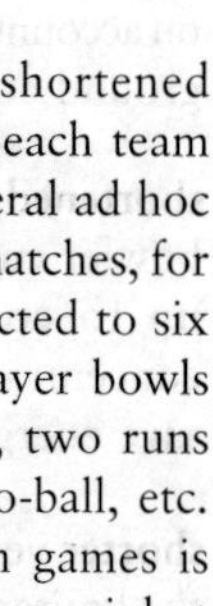

umpire's signal for six

number of runs that can be scored off a single delivery. A sixer shot is always dramatic and exciting to watch and marks the limit of triumph for a batsman against a bowler's delivery.

skid A delivery that comes off the pitch faster and lower than normal. Skidding is caused by the nature of the wicket, as also by the unique action of a bowler.

skier A well connected, powerful shot, hit very high into the deep field.

skipper The captain of a team; the player appointed to lead the side.

skittle (said of a team) To be all out for a low score due to effective bowling and fielding.

slant A delivery angled across the batsman or across the wicket. Bowlers often use the width of the bowling crease to gain a sharper angle and surprise the batsman with the variation.

sledging Loud or unsavoury comments made by close-in fielders to unsettle the batsman. Australian cricketers are notorious for using this tactic, even though it is considered against the code of conduct for the game.

sleeve The tubular rubber covering on the handle of a bat meant to improve grip and comfort.

slice (sliced shot) An aggressive back-foot stroke resembling a cut in which the bat is angled upwards to hit the ball high up towards point or third man.

sliding stop A skilful piece of fielding in which the fielder intercepts a ball travelling away from him by slipping to the ground in a swift, sliding motion.

sling action An unusual bowling action resembling a slanted arm slung over the shoulder, as distinct from the more common high-arm or round-arm action. (Australian fast bowler Jeff Thompson – one of the fastest bowlers in the game – bowled with a sling action.)

sling action

slip An important off-side catching position behind the batsman, and between wicket-keeper and gully. Depending upon the width away from the wicket-keeper, slip positions are further classified as first, second and third slips. The distance between any two slip positions is about 2–3 yards, and the depth varies according to the pace of the bowler or type of pitch.

slip cordon Ring of slip fielders placed around the batsman. In an extreme attacking situation, up to five fielders could be positioned in the slip cordon – from leg slip to third slip – in anticipation of a catch.

slip fielder Normally refers to any of the slip fielders from first slip to third slip, but may also include the leg slip. A slip fielder is noted for his ability to anticipate and hold sharp catches coming from the edge of the bat.

slip fielder

slog A mighty swipe at the ball, intending to dispatch it to the ropes. Although lacking in precision, and often premeditated, a slog is always played with power and aggression, especially when quick run scoring is required.

slog overs The last few overs of an innings in a one-day match when the batting tempo is increased in an attempt to score as many runs as possible. Thus, these overs are noted for batsmen playing a higher number of attacking and risky shots, which also results in quicker dismissals.

slogger A batsman taking mighty swipes at the bowling, often cross-batted and lacking in finesse. Although risky and inconsistent, the utility of a slogger's knock lies in the quick runs scored and the unsettling of the opposition.

slot *(1)* Position for a particular type of player in the team, like an opening slot or an all-rounder's slot. *(2)* A spot on the pitch ideal for the batsman to play a shot or ideal for the bowler to attack.

slow bowler Any right- or left-arm spinner, bowling slow off-spin, leg-spin, or similar deliveries.

slow left-arm Orthodox type of spin bowling by a left-arm spinner, with the ball turning from leg to off for a right-handed batsman. Spin is imparted by the use of fingers (rather than wrist), like for right-arm, off-spin bowling. Also referred to as left-arm orthodox spin.

slow mover *(1)* A fielder lacking in anticipation and speed when fielding a ball, thus prone to conceding additional runs. *(2)* A batsman at the wicket who does not take his runs fast enough. See *slow runner.*

slow outfield A ground where the ball travels to the fence slowly due to thick grass, or sandy patches, making it difficult for the batsman to score boundaries.

slow over-rate The time taken to bowl an over varies mainly according to the type of bowler (fast, or slow), although other factors, like the manner of scoring by the batsmen, also have a bearing. At higher levels of cricket, bowling 15 to 16 six-ball overs per hour is considered an average over-rate, and 14 or less is considered a slow over-rate.

slow pitch A wicket on which the ball loses pace after pitching. While offering no assistance to the bowler, a slow wicket is also not conducive to strokeplay, thus making it difficult for batsmen to score runs freely. Also referred to as a slow wicket or slow track.

slow runner A batsman who does not exhibit adequate speed and sharpness in taking runs. This often impairs his judgement of runs causing him to hesitate before taking them.

slow scoring A relative term indicating that the batting side is taking longer or using more overs, to score runs than expected.

slower one (slower ball) A ball delivered at a slower pace than the normal deliveries in an attempt to deceive the batsman into mistiming his stroke. It is more effectively deployed by fast and medium fast bowlers than spin bowlers.

small ground A cricket ground where the average distance from the pitch to the boundary line is closer to the stipulated minimum of 60 yards. (Note: cricket grounds can be of varying sizes, as the distance from the pitch to the boundary line is permitted to be between 60 and 90 yards.)

smash A powerful, unrestrained shot by the batsman, executed with a full flow of the bat.

snap A sharp catch taken by a close-in fielder.

snick A thinly connected shot with the ball taking the edge of the bat and travelling, often uppishly, to any of the positions behind the batsman.

snip back A delivery that turns or cuts sharply or unexpectedly into the batsman, forcing him to play a hurried stroke.

soft hands A careful and defensive stroke, executed with the least amount of force, so that the ball does not carry to the fielders.

soft hands

specialist A player who is included in the team to perform a specialist function like batting (opening, or middle), bowling (fast, medium pace, or spin) or wicket-keeping. Players also specialise in fielding at certain positions (slips, point, etc.), but are rarely included in the team for their fielding skills alone.

specialist fielder A fielder possessing the expert skills for fielding at a particular position, e.g., a fielder may be a specialist slip fielder.

spectacles Said of a batsman who is dismissed for duck in both the innings of a match, because the two zeros scored are figuratively compared to a pair of spectacles.

speed gun An electronic gadget that measures and displays the speed of fast moving objects. The gadget is optionally deployed during important international cricket matches to measure the bowling speed, particularly when the line-up for the match includes some reputed fast bowlers.

speed merchant See *speedster.*

speedster A specialist fast or fast medium bowler.

spell The number of overs bowled consecutively by a bowler from one end.

spikers Special boots with metal points fitted to the soles, worn mainly by fast bowlers to avoid skidding.

spill To drop a catch.

spin The rotation imparted to a ball to cause it to turn after pitching. It is achieved by gripping the ball in a particular way and using the force of fingers or roll of wrists, at the moment of delivery. See *off-spin* and *leg-spin.*

spinner A slow bowler who employs flight and spin to make his bowling effective. Spinners are principally of two types, finger-spinners and wrist-spinners.

spinner's paradise A wicket on which spinners get all the help – sharp turn and varying bounce – and batsmen find run scoring, even survival, very difficult.

spinning wicket A wicket that helps spinners by providing an appreciable turn.

splice Lower part of the handle, connected to the blade of the bat through a 'v'-shaped cut.

spoon a catch (said of a batsman) To offer an easy catch in an attempt to play a stroke; to fall prey to the bowler's guiles and hit the ball into the hands of a fielder.

sporting wicket A pitch that provides extra pace or bounce to fast bowlers to work skilfully and exploit it.

spread-eagled A batsman comprehensively bowled out, with the stumps tilting in different directions.

spreadout field Denotes a defensive field setting with fielders mostly placed in the deep with hardly anyone in catching positions.

square Part of the field or field positions, along an imaginary extended line from the batting crease on either side of the wicket.

square cut

square cut An attacking off-side stroke played with a horizontal swing of the bat, hitting the ball square of the wicket. The ideal delivery for a square cut is one pitched short of length, passing outside the off-stump.

square drive A modified drive played with the bat flowing at an angle, hitting it between point and cover point. Ideally played to balls outside the off-stump, both off the front foot and back foot, the square drive is an authoritative and graceful shot, but is best executed when the batsman is well set.

square leg A fielding position on the leg-side, in line with the batting crease. The normal square-leg position is 25–30 yards away from the batsman. Its variation are short square leg, which is closer to the pitch, and deep square leg, which is closer to the boundary.

square-leg umpire See *leg umpire.*

square-up Body and feet movement by the batsman to turn and face the bowler directly, to play a delivery defensively or to leave it alone.

squat *(1)* A delivery that has a lower than normal bounce after pitching short of good length. *(2)* The bent-knee position adopted by the wicket-keeper and close-in fielders in readiness to catch or field the ball.

stance

stance The manner in which a batsman stands at the wicket and holds his bat in readiness to face a delivery.

stand *(1 batting)* A partnership between two batsman in an innings, measured in terms of number of runs added to the total. *(2 umpiring)* To perform the duties of an umpire in a match.

stand-up To keep wickets by standing close to the stumps (as for a spinner), as distinct from standing several yards behind (as for fast bowlers).

steal a single Said of a batsman who takes a quick run by confusing a fielder, when it is apparently a no-run situation or it is impossible to take one.

steer A controlled, wristy stroke, deflecting the ball neatly behind square, using the pace and bounce of the delivery to good effect.

step-out Said of a batsman who comes out of the crease to play a delivery, mostly hitting it on the half-volley or full toss.

stick *(1)* A stump or one of the three wooden rods making the wicket. *(2)* A sharp catch resting itself in the fielders hands on reflex action rather than with the fielder making a conscious effort to hold the catch.

sticker A very defensive batsman who prefers to take his own time to score, keeping survival rather than scoring runs as his main motive. This style of batting is more relevant for the longer version of the game than for one-day matches.

sticky wicket A pitch affected by rain on which the ball bounces or turns unpredictably, thus making batting very difficult.

stock bowler A bowler used for long spells, mainly to control run scoring and give the strike bowlers a chance to rest. Stock bowlers are better known for their accuracy and stamina than for their attacking qualities.

stock delivery The normal delivery of a bowler, bowled with emphasis on line and length, rather than attack or variation.

stonewall Said of a batsman who plays in a totally defensive manner, aiming to occupy the crease for as long as possible and scoring his runs at an extremely slow pace. A predominantly defensive batsman is, thus, called a stonewaller.

stop To intercept a moving ball and prevent it from travelling further. It denotes an abrupt action, as opposed to fielding, which denotes a more skilful performance.

straight Area of the pitch or field directly in front of the batsman, extending up to the boundary line.

straight-arm delivery A delivery bowled with the arm straightening up just before releasing the ball, instead of completing a proper roll of the arm. A straight arm delivery is considered unfair and is declared a no-ball. See also *chuck*.

straight-bat stroke A stroke played with the bat held perpendicular and moving in a straight line with the delivery. It signifies a safe and polished way of batting, as opposed to playing cross bat or across the line, which are the riskier forms.

straight drive A powerful drive passing close to the bowler or over his head, to the area straight in front of the batsman.

straight drive

straighter one A variation delivery of a spinner that goes straight through after pitching instead of taking the expected turn.

strategy A longer term game plan – covering an innings, match or the entire series – employed by the captain of a team to achieve specific goals.

streaky shot An edgy shot deflecting the ball into the area behind the batsman. Generally the result of an imperfect stroke, it can also be played intentionally by improvising a defensive stroke.

strike *(1 bowling)* To dismiss the batsman with the delivery. *(2 batting)* To hit the ball firmly in a somewhat unconventional style; to face the bowling.

strike bowler One of the main bowlers in the team who is expected to take wickets with attacking deliveries bowled in short spells.

strike rate *(1 bowling)* Performance measure for a bowler, indicating wickets captured per hundred balls, or average number of balls used to take a wicket. *(2 batting)* Performance measure for a batsman, indicating runs scored per hundred balls, or runs scored as a percentage of the number of balls faced.

striker The batsman whose turn it is to face the bowling, as opposed to the batsman who is at the other end (non-striker) of the pitch.

strip The playing surface in the centre of the ground. See also *pitch* or *wicket.*

stroke The act of playing a ball with due emphasis on skill and finesse, aiming to minimise the risk of dismissal while maximising effectiveness. A stroke is distinct from a 'shot', which primarily aims at hitting the ball with power.

stroke sheet A sheet with a circular chart, on which the batsman's scoring shots during an innings are analysed by showing the direction of strokes and runs scored in it. See *wagon wheel.*

strokeless Said of a batsman who is unable to play strokes for a given time or against a given bowler; one who is completely on the defensive.

strokeplay A composite term for a variety of batting strokes played with skill, grace and good timing.

strokeplayer A batsman reputed for playing a wide range of attractive strokes.

strong arm Said of a fielder who regularly sends in fast and accurate returns from the deep field.

stump *(1)* The three wooden rods that, together with the bails on top, comprise a wicket. Each wooden rod, or stump, stands 28 inches above the ground and is dome shaped and grooved at the top to hold the bail. The three stumps are equally spaced from one another and cover a total width of 9 inches. *(2)* To dismiss a batsman by stumping, i.e. with the wicket-keeper dislodging the bails, as the batsman misses playing a delivery while being out of his ground.

stump

stump vision A very close vision of batting and bowling action captured through a miniature camera fitted into the off-stump. Its main practical use is to show television action replays. However, as the system is not easy to install or maintain, it is only used during the telecasting of important matches.

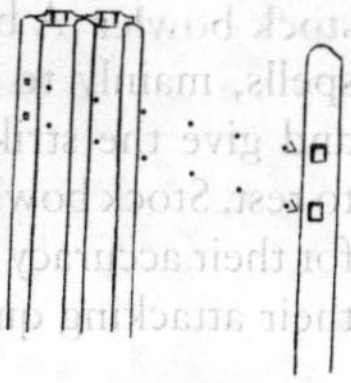

stump vision

stumper A term used to describe a wicket-keeper renowned for stumping. The usage of this term is now obsolete as the number of dismissals through stumping are relatively few.

stumping (stumped) A mode of dismissal in which the wicket-keeper quickly gathers the ball and dislodges the bails as the batsman misses playing a delivery while being out of his ground.

substitute (substitute fielder) One of the reserve players called in to field in place of a regular player who is injured during the match, or is unwell. A substitute fielder is not permitted to bowl, bat or keep wickets. Traditionally substitute fielders are also not placed in specialist fielding positions.

substitute ball Replacement for a ball that is lost or loses shape during play. The substitute ball is roughly similar to the original in terms of the use and wear and tear. See *replacement ball.*

substitute runner Subject to permission by the opposing captain, a substitute runner is allowed for a batsman who is injured or becomes unwell while at the crease and wishes to continue batting. Where possible, the substitute runner should be a dismissed batsman and should wear protective equipment similar to that of the batsman for whom the substitute is required.

suicidal run A risky run attempted, resulting or nearly resulting in a run out.

suicidal shot A reckless and injudicious stroke, almost certainly resulting in a dismissal.

Sunday League Short for John Player Sunday League, the premiere limited-overs championship in England. Started in 1969, the official name subsequently changed to AXA Life League, although it continues to be commonly known as Sunday League. Matches in this league are limited to forty overs a side and are played on Sunday afternoons between the English county teams.

sundries Extras; run(s) added to the total on account of byes, leg-byes, wides and no-balls. In Australia and New Zealand, the term sundries is preferred to extras.

supporting role (said of a batsman) A restrained knock, played with the objective of letting the senior batting partner take most of the strike and do the bulk of the scoring.

surface Refers to the playing surface, i.e. wicket or pitch.

suspect action Bowling action that is not always clean or perfect; bowling action which is occasionally jerky or has an element of chucking.

suspension Unlike in football or hockey, in cricket errant players are not suspended while the game is in progress. However, where appropriate, a warning is given by the umpire and further aberrations are dealt with more sternly. A player found guilty may be suspended from a future match or matches, following a post match review of the incidents.

sweep An attacking leg-side shot played by going down on one knee and hitting the ball with a low cross-batted swing. The shot is mostly played against spinners' deliveries pitched on or outside the leg stump, hitting the ball between square-leg and fine leg.

sweep

sweeper A fielder positioned in the deep to cover a large area along the boundary line. The chosen fielder is necessarily one who can move fast and execute a quick pick-up and throw. The two main sweeper positions are **sweeper cover,** fielding along the cover boundary, and **sweeper mid-wicket,** fielding along the mid-wicket boundary.

swerve The lateral movement of the ball in the air; the same as swing, but obsolete.

swing The sideways movement or curve in the trajectory of a delivery before it reaches the batsman. Apart from special bowling skills, the newness of the ball and weather conditions also influence swing bowling. A good swing makes it difficult for the batsman to negotiate the delivery. See also *inswing, outswing.*

swing and miss An unsuccessful attempt by a batsman at playing an attacking shot.

swinger A delivery bowled as an inswinger or an outswinger.

grip for bowling a swinger

synthetic turf Artificial wicket. Such wickets are mainly used for staging show matches where a regular cricket ground/pitch is not available.

T t

tactics Specific manoeuvres used in a situation to get the upper hand on the opposition, like changing the batting order, setting an attacking field, etc.

tail The last few batsmen in a team's innings, consisting of players (mainly bowlers) who are not expected to contribute much to the team's total.

tail-ender A player not reputed for good batting skills and sent in to bat towards the latter part of the innings. Tail-enders are usually specialist bowlers, but may include a wicket-keeper if his batting is weak.

tail-up A bowler bowling with extra zeal and fire, especially after taking a wicket or two and aiming for further strikes.

tail wagging A productive and prolonged batting display by the last few unrecognised batsmen or tail-enders, resulting in a good number of runs being added to the total.

take *(1 wicket-keeper)* To receive a delivery neatly in the gloves after it is missed, left alone or snicked by the batsman. *(2 wicket-keeper/fielder)* To receive a throw from a fielder, as when attempting to run out the batsman. *(3 bowler)* To capture the stated number of wickets.

take a start Forward movement by a fielder, or non-striker batsman, along with the bowler's run-up in order to build up momentum for running.

take the cap off Gesture by a batsman to acknowledge the applause for reaching an individual batting milestone, like fifty or a century.

taking guard The elaborate action of a batsman in checking his position for stance with the umpire and marking it with a piece of chalk or in any other appropriate manner. See *guard*.

tall over An over in which many runs are scored, compared to the average scoring rate. The term is used in the context of a bar chart plotting the team's run rate, wherein an expensive over appears like a tall building. See also *Manhattan*.

tap A gentle cross-batted shot, played off the back foot, to a ball on or outside the off-stump. The stroke is seldom strong enough to fetch a boundary, but can be effectively used to place the ball for one or two runs over a wide area between extra cover and backward point.

target Total to be achieved for victory by the team batting last.

team physio A qualified physiotherapist assigned to the team to attend to players' injuries and fitness problems. International teams find the services of a team physio indispensable and he is commonly included as a permanent member of the support squad that accompanies the team on its tours.

television umpire See *third umpire*.

ten-wicket haul The instance of a bowler taking a total of ten or more wickets in the two innings of a match. Like a century for a batsman, a ten-wicket haul is a measure of achievement for the bowler. Also referred to as ten wickets in a match.

test centre Town or city where test matches are held or at least one test match was held in the recent past. There are presently over 80 test centres world-wide.

test debut The first test of a player's career, giving him the honour of representing his country.

test-playing nation One of the ten test-playing countries recognised by the ICC, viz., Australia, Bangladesh England, India, Pakistan, South Africa, Sri Lanka, West Indies and Zimbabwe.

test (test match) A match at the highest level of cricket, played between any two full members of the ICC. Test matches are typically scheduled to last five days and imply that the true mettle of players will be tested in a game played to international standards.

The Don Short for Sir Donald Bradman, the greatest batsman the game has ever seen. See *Bradman.*

thick outfield A ground or part of the ground, with a heavy growth of grass which impedes the ball from travelling at normal speed to the boundary.

think out(said of a bowler) To identify a batsman's weak point and bowl to a plan to get him out.

thinking captain A captain who implements well thought out strategies during a match, fine tuned to individual players and evolving situations that keep the opposition under pressure.

third man An off-side fielding position behind the batsman, placed deep enough to cover strokes going through gully and third slip. Mainly a defensive fielding position, the third man is normally able to cover a larger area of the field between backward point and behind the slips.

third slip A catching position on the off-side, placed between gully and second slip. It is deployed when fast or medium fast bowlers are operating, particularly with a new ball.

third umpire An additional umpire, besides the two main umpires, who watches the game from outside the field. His job is to study the television replays and adjudicate those cases that are referred to him by the main umpires. These cases, typically, include appeals for run outs and stumpings, as well as borderline cases for fours and sixes which the main umpires cannot see clearly.

signal by a main umpire, asking for a third umpire's decision

thirty-yard circle A circle drawn around the pitch, at a radius of thirty yards. In one-day matches only two fielders can be placed outside this circle, during the first fifteen overs of an innings.

thrash*(1 batsman)* To strike a powerful hit or score freely through a series of attacking shots. *(2 bowler)* To come under attack by a batsman and concede many runs. *(3 team)* To defeat the opposing team by a very large margin.

three-figure mark The milestone of scoring one hundred or more runs by a batsman, two batsmen in a partnership or by the team, as stated. See *century.*

throat The upper most part of the bat where the handle connects with the blade.

throat ball A delivery that rises sharply up to a batsman's throat and forces him to play a defensive or evasive stroke; similar to a bumper, but always well directed.

through bat and pad A bowler's delivery passing through the gap between the bat and front pad of the batsman as he shapes to play a stroke. The situation marks a triumph for the bowler as the batsman is often hopelessly beaten or very narrowly escapes being bowled or stumped. Also known as through the gate.

through the gate (through bat and pad) See *gate*.

throw

throw *(1)* Return sent in by a fielder when in possession of the ball. *(2)* An unfair bowling action in which the bowler straightens the bowling arm just before delivery, instead of bowling with a full and proper roll of the arm. See also *chuck*.

throw caution to the winds To bat in a very risky manner, hitting out boldly without fear of dismissal.

throw out A return by a fielder (bowler and wicket-keeper included), which hits the stumps directly, resulting in a run out dismissal.

throwing arm The stronger hand of a fielder used for sending returns.

thump To hit the ball with authority, applying maximum power and good timing.

tidy over An over in which a bowler maintains a good line and length and gives few opportunities to the batsman to play shots.

tie *(1)* A match that ends with both teams scoring exactly the same number of runs, provided the team batting last is all out. If the team batting last is not all out, then the match is considered a draw. *(2)* A match or fixture between two teams.

tied down Said of a batsman who is unable to score runs at an appreciable rate due to tight bowling, sharp fielding and precise field setting.

tight bowling A spell of accurate and economical bowling, generally from both ends, giving few run scoring opportunities to the batsmen.

tight over An over in which the batsmen are unable to play productive strokes, resulting in few runs being scored.

timber Also known as stump, though this usage is rare; called 'timber' because the stumps are made of wood.

time in/out An entry on the scoresheet recording the starting and ending time of a batsman's or team's innings in order to determine the time (hours/minutes) taken to compile the score.

timed out A provision under the Laws of Cricket whereby a new batsman may be declared out by the umpire, upon appeal by the opposing team, if he takes longer than two minutes to come to the crease. However, this provision exists only as a deterrent and has never been applied in practice.

timeless test Refers to the final test match at Durban of the 1938/39 series between South Africa and England. As the series was still open, it was decided to play this test match to finish regardless of the time taken. However, a definitive result could not be achieved even until tea on the tenth day of the test when rain interrupted play. The game was called-off at this stage, declaring the result a draw, to enable the English side to rush to Cape Town to catch a ship back home. This is still the longest first-class match ever played as well as one in which a record (since broken only twice) 1,981 runs were scored. [Brief scores: South Africa 530 and 481; England 316 and 654 for five.]

timing The batsman's skill in playing shots at the precise moment from the middle part of the bat, so that the ball is dispatched effectively without use of much force.

toe smasher A relatively new term for a fast yorker aimed at the batsman's toes. It often results in the batsman having to play a hurried or evasive stroke to avoid getting into trouble.

ton A score of one hundred or more runs by an individual batsman. See also *century* or *hundred.*

top bailer A delivery that bounces to the top of the stumps and is accurate enough to dislodge the bails, or nearly do so.

top-edge A misconnected shot in which the ball touches the upper edge of the bat and goes high up in the air, upwards to the wicket-keeper or the slips.

top order The first half of the batting line-up, comprising the two opening batsmen and those following up to numbers 5 or 6. These are the players included in the side for their specialist batting skills.

top score *(1)* The highest individual score of a batsman at a given level of cricket, during a specified period or during his entire career. *(2)* The highest contribution of runs by an individual batsman in a team's innings.

top-spin Straight spin imparted on a delivery so that the ball does not turn but hurries to the batsman upon pitching.

top-spinner A top-spin delivery, mostly bowled by wrist spinners to surprise the batsman, who may expect it to turn or bounce in the normal way.

toppie (toppy) An Australian term coined by the legendary leg-spinner Shane Warne to mean top-spinner. See *top-spinner.*

toss The flip of the coin before the commencement of a match by the captains of the two teams. The winning captain has the right to decide whether his team will bat or field (bowl) first.

total The aggregate score of a team during an innings, comprising the individual scores of all the batsmen and the extras.

touch A player's current form or effectiveness in batting or bowling.

tour A visit by a team to place(s) away from home to play one or more pre-arranged matches.

toying with the bowling Situation in which a batsman has complete ascendancy over the bowlers and scores freely, hitting or placing the ball at will.

track The central strip in the ground used for batting and bowling. Also known as pitch.

trademark shot A batsman's favourite shot, played in a unique style. For example, Sachin Tendular's straight drive or Brian Lara's flick to square leg.

training camp A specially arranged practice and coaching session for a longish period (for one or more weeks) to improve the skills and effectiveness of the players.

trap To confuse a batsman into playing or attempting a stroke that causes his dismissal, e.g. to trap in the leg-side field.

triangular series A series of one-day international matches played between three teams on a round-robin basis.

trick A premeditated move to confuse or outwit the opposing batsman or bowler.

triple century A score of three hundred, or more runs by an individual batsman- a monumental achievement at any level of cricket.

true wicket A pitch that gives fair opportunities to bowlers and batsmen and behaves quite predictably over the entire duration of the game. A true test wicket normally assists fast bowlers in the early part, batsmen in the longish middle part and spinners in the later part, without ever predominantly favouring either the bowlers or the batsmen.

trundler A bowler, generally a spinner or medium pacer.

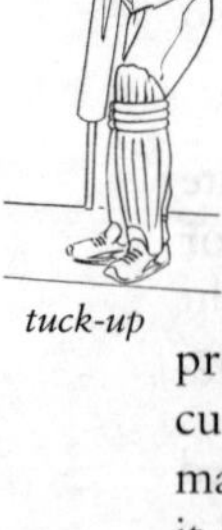

tuck-up

tuck-up To be restricted for space when playing a stroke due to a sharp deviation or unexpected rise in the delivery upon pitching, particularly with the ball coming into the batsman.

turf wicket A wicket prepared of the natural soil, through a technical process involving constant watering, curing, mowing and rolling. All test matches are played on turf wickets, and it is quite unusual now for a one-day international or even a first-class match, to be played on anything other than a turf wicket.

turn *(1)* Change in the direction of a delivery upon pitching, due to the spin imparted on it by the bowler. *(2)* Quality of the wicket in terms of its responsiveness to spin bowling.

turner A wicket on which the ball turns appreciably; a wicket known to help spinners.

turning pitch A pitch on which the ball turns appreciably, thus helping spinners. Quality of soil, curing and preparation technique determine the extent of turn offered in a wicket. Normal wickets too may start turning at a later stage of the game, particularly in tests or first-class matches, due to wear and tear.

two-eyed stance A stance in which the batsman faces the bowler with open chest and shoulders pointing in the square direction, while the body remains bent over the bat as in the normal stance.

two-eyed stance

U u

umbrella field An attacking field setting for fast bowlers, with many fielders placed in an arc behind the batsman. Apart from the wicket-keeper, it includes positions like leg slip, short leg, gully and up to four slips.

umpire One of the two officials on the ground responsible for conducting the game in accordance with the Laws of Cricket and other applicable match/ tournament rules. The main functions of an umpire are, to adjudicate appeals for the dismissal of a batsman, declare fours/sixers, signal byes/leg-byes and wides/no-balls, call overs, dead balls, etc.

umpire's inspection Assessment of the playing conditions (state of the pitch, ground, light, etc.) by the umpires in order to determine whether or not the game can commence. This is particularly done after rain, or bad light has interrupted play, and the conditions have improved just enough to consider resuming the game.

unbeaten *(1 batsman)* Batsman not dismissed or remaining not out in the innings. *(2 team)* A team that has not lost a match in the series, tournament, or over a stated period of time.

unconventional shot An unusual shot played under the demands of a situation or on account of the individual flair and preference of the batsman.

underarm bowling A form of bowling in which the arm is rolled back and the ball delivered from below waist height. This form of bowling is now out of favour and the overarm action is used exclusively in all forms of cricket.

underarm throw

underarm throw To return the ball with the throwing arm moving at around middle body level, rather than at, or above, shoulder level.

underpitch A delivery landing a little short of good length, thus, relatively easier for the batsman to play.

unfair play Any act, or behaviour by the players that goes against the accepted norms and traditions of the game, even if not specifically covered under the game rules; e.g., sledging or ball-tampering.

unlucky Said of a player who misses an opportunity or fails to reach an individual milestone due to faulty judgement by the umpire, errors committed by teammates or simply due to the game situation.

unplayable Exceptionally effective bowling or adverse playing conditions (poor light, unpredictable wicket, etc.) which make it extremely difficult for the batsman to face the bowling and survive.

unprotected area A part of the field left unmanned or out of the reach of fielders.

unsighted A player, or umpire on the field unable to respond to the situation due to another player momentarily blocking his vision.

unwritten law Traditions of the game falling outside the stricter code of law, yet expected to be followed by the players. These traditions mostly cover the behavioural aspects of play, such as not bowling bouncers to tail-enders, etc.

up Part of the pitch closer to the batsman. See *pitch up*.

upper cut A cut played to a rising ball outside the off-stump, hitting it over the slips or gully fielders. As for other cut shots, the bat moves horizontally, but the blade is angled upwards to make the ball fly off upon impact.

upper hand The top hand gripping the handle. Its function is to guide the direction and flow of the bat, while the bottom hand imparts force.

uppish A shot going up in the air at a catchable height.

upright stance

upright stance A manner of stance in which the batsman faces the bowler with open shoulders and semi-erect body. This contrasts with the normal stance in which the body is bent over the bat, with the front shoulder pointing towards the bowler.

utility batsman A batsman who can be sent in to bat at any position – opening, middle order, or late order – in the absence of a more established batsman. Although not a specialist at any of these positions, he can be expected to bat competently and contribute moderately.

utility player An all-rounder who can fit into various roles and perform several functions competently, such as operate as the main bowler or support bowler, bat as an opener or lower order batsman, and field well in any position. A utility player is, however, not considered a true specialist in any discipline of the game.

V v

V Area in front of the batsman, between wide mid-off and wide mid-on. Straight lines drawn from the batsman to these extreme points form a 'V' shape. Playing straight-bat strokes within the 'V' area is an ideal way for a new batsman to start building up his innings.

variation Subtle changes deployed by a bowler from one delivery to another in an attempt to force the batsman into making an error. It is achieved by changing the various elements of a delivery, such as angle, pace, swing, flight and turn.

variety *(1 team)* Refers to the different types of specialist bowlers – e.g. fast, medium pace, leg-spin, off-spin, left-arm – present in a team. *(2 bowler)* A range of different deliveries used by a bowler to dismiss or unsettle the batsman; e.g., a leg-spinner mixing googlies, flippers and top-spinners with his normal leg-spin deliveries.

veteran's cricket Matches organised exclusively for veteran cricketers. These are mostly one-day internationals with specified selection criteria (e.g. age above 35 years), but following all other normal cricket rules.

vice-captain A player appointed to take over the team's leadership when the regular captain is not available. He is also consulted on various matters relating to game strategy and team selection.

victory margin A measure to quantify the extent of victory achieved, which is mainly of one of two types, *(i)* by the number of remaining wickets, if the batting team achieves the target, and *(ii)* by the surplus number of runs scored if the fielding team restricts the batting team to a lower total. Additionally, an innings victory is also possible in the longer version of the game. See also *innings defeat/ victory*.

visor The moveable front portion of a helmet which protects the face.

volley A delivery that reaches the batsman before hitting the ground, but not high enough to be a full toss. It is one of the easier deliveries for the batsman to hit.

W w

wagon wheel A circular chart plotting the run scoring strokes played by a batsman during an innings. The completed chart looks like a wagon wheel, with lines drawn from the wickets towards the boundary representing the direction of strokes. Runs scored are also indicated against each corresponding line. See also *strokesheet*.

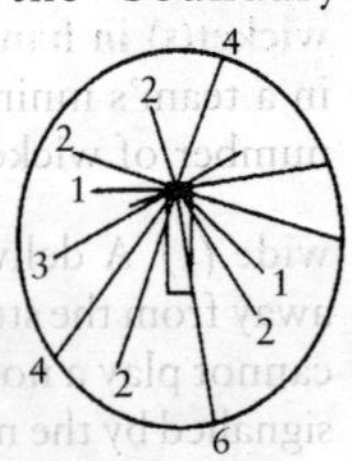

wagon wheel

walk Said of a batsman who leaves the crease upon being dismissed to a thin edge catch, without waiting for the umpire to uphold the appeal.

walk-over A situation where the match is awarded to a team, either because the opposing team does not turn up or refuses to play.

walking back to the pavilion Expression conveying that the batsman is just dismissed. The other popular variation of this expression is, back in the pavilion, which denotes the wicket(s) fallen.

walking run A comfortable run, completed by the batsmen walking rather than running, after the ball is played to the deep field.

warning Umpires warn players whose actions on the field go against the code of ethics for the conduct of the game, e.g., sledging, unduly hostile bowling, running on the pitch, etc.

washed-out Match abandoned during the scheduled time due to rain with little or no play possible.

wasted delivery A harmless ball bowled wide of the stumps – particularly in a critical situation – which the batsman easily lets go.

well bowled A commonly used phrase appreciating the bowler's effort in bowling an effective delivery or spell which causes the batsman some difficulty in playing it.

well-judged catch A high catch taken in the mid-field or deep-field with good anticipation and quick movement towards the dropping ball.

well set Said of a batsman or a pair of batsmen, playing comfortably after having got a good measure of the bowling attack and the nature of the wicket.

wet patch A small, partially affected area on the pitch due to rain water seeping through the covers. A delivery pitched in this area often behaves unpredictably, thus causing problems to batsmen.

wet pitch A pitch affected by rain or moisture seeping through the covers, thus playing unpredictably and making batting very difficult.

whack A clean and powerful shot played by the batsman.

white ball The white cricket ball used in day–night (one-day) matches to improve visibility under floodlights.

whitewash A test or one-day international series victory by one team outplaying the other by a 5–0, or similar margin. The term is more aptly used in the context of the victory of a white cricketing nation. See also *blackwash*.

wicket *(1)* Also known as pitch, i.e. the strip of playing area at the centre of the ground used for batting and bowling. *(2)* The set of three stumps (including the two bails) at either end of the pitch. *(3)* The playing life of a batsman in an innings; thus, 'to loose a wicket' means to be out or be dismissed. *(4)* The dismissal of a batsman by a bowler or by the fielding team. *(5)* Part of the score of a team in an innings, indicating the number of batsmen dismissed for the given score, e.g., 100 for two wickets.

wicket-keeper A fielder who stands behind the stumps to perform various specialist functions, like stumping, collecting deliveries not played by the batsman, taking catches, receiving returns from fielders, etc. The wicket-keeper is always busily involved in the game and is the only one from the fielding side allowed to wear pads and gloves. Also referred to as glove(s)man.

wicket-keeper

wicket-keeper batsman A wicket-keeper with a strong batting ability, nearly as good as that of a regular batsman. Also referred to as wicket-keeper all-rounder.

wicket-keeper's pads Special pads worn by a wicket-keeper. These pads are shorter and more loosely tied to help the frequent bending and squatting movements of a wicket-keeper. See *pads.*

wicket-keeper's pads

wicket-keeping gloves Special, extra large and extra padded gloves worn by the wicket-keeper to stop or catch the ball.

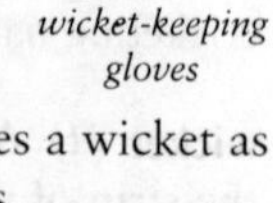
wicket-keeping gloves

wicket maiden An over in which the bowler takes a wicket as well as concedes no runs.

wicket-to-wicket Tight, good length bowling in straight line with the wickets, allowing little room for the batsmen to score runs.

wicketless Said of a bowler who fails to capture a wicket over a specified period, e.g., 'wicketless in the match'.

wicket(s) in hand Remaining wickets in a team's innings, i.e. ten minus the number of wickets fallen.

wide *(1)* A delivery bowled so much away from the stumps that the batsman cannot play a normal stroke. A wide is signalled by the main umpire spreading both the arms horizontally. The delivery is considered invalid and the bowler must bowl an extra one to compensate. For each wide delivery, one 'wide' run is added to the extras, but if more than one run is taken by the batsmen, those are counted too. This rule is implemented more strictly in one-day matches than in first-class matches, particularly for balls pitching outside the leg stump. *(2)* A term denoting that the associated fielding position is placed a few paces closer to the square area, as compared to the corresponding normal position, e.g., wide mid-off, wide mid-on, wide gully, etc.

umpire's signal for wide

wild throw A fast and off-target return from a fielder, making it difficult for the wicket-keeper or the receiver to stop the ball.

willow The special wood from which cricket bats are made. The best willow trees are found mainly in England. A cricket bat is also sometimes referred to as a 'willow', identifying it with the willow tree.

wind The breeze blowing across the ground. Bowlers often find it helpful to bowl with the wind to get extra movement in the air.

Windies The West Indies are known as the Windies.

Wisden Cricket Almanac A famous publication from England providing extensive coverage of English cricket. It also provides scores/reports of test and one-day international matches, as well as coverage of important regional matches played in other parts of the world. Published annually since 1864, the book abounds in records and statistics and is a major source of reference for cricket information.

Wisden Cricketer of the Year A prestigious award for individual cricketers, instituted by the publishers of the *Wisden Cricket Almanac*. Every year five cricketers are selected for the award, based upon their performances in the preceding English cricket season.

women's cricket General term for matches or tournaments at various levels involving women's cricket teams.

work around A manner of cautious batting in which runs are scored in singles and twos by placing the ball into gaps, using the pace and turn of the delivery to good effect.

workhorse A bowler who shoulders the brunt of the team's bowling attack; a bowler often relied upon to bowl long spells.

World Cup The cricket world cup of one-day matches played once every four years. Begun in 1975, the tournament is played on a league cum knock-out basis and involves all the test-playing nations and the top three or four associate member nations. The 1999 World Cup was the seventh such tournament. It was played in England and won by Australia.

A World Cup

worm graph A line graph that plots the team total at the end of every over in a one-day match. It illustrates how the team total has progressed, in relation to overs faced, at various stages of the match. The graph is produced with the use of computer graphics and is intermittently shown during television coverage of the match as visual support to the commentary.

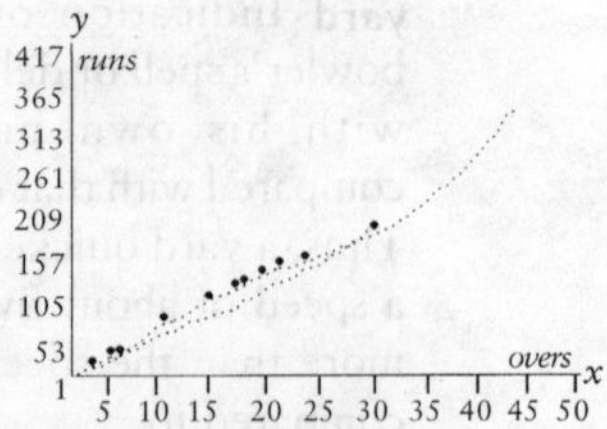

worm graph

worth a shout An appeal for dismissal (for lbw, caught behind or a close catch) not upheld by the umpire, but close enough to be worth trying for.

wrist spinner A bowler who delivers the ball with a roll of the wrists, like a right-arm leg-spinner.

wrist-work *(batting)* Deft and skilful strokes executed with the use of wrist and timing rather than brute force. Batsmen who rely mainly on wristy shots are, thus, elegant to watch.

wristy Strokes played with a reliance on wrist-work, as opposed to shots played with arm power or with a full swing of the bat.

wrong foot bowling For normal bowling, the leg opposite the bowling hand takes the final stride. In wrong foot bowling, the leg as well as the bowling hand are on the same side.

wrong hand (wrong arm) The weaker of the two hands; the hand not used to throw the ball.

wrong 'un (wrong one) A spinner's delivery which, upon pitching, turns in the direction opposite to the one his action might suggest, e.g., a googly.

Y y

yard Indication of the speed of a bowler's spell or delivery as compared with his own normal speed or compared with that of another bowler. Thus, a yard quicker or slower means a speed of about five per cent less or more than the speed of bowling it is compared to.

yorker A full length delivery pitching near the batsman's block hole and aimed at passing underneath the bat to hit the stumps. Normally bowled by fast or medium fast bowlers, a yorker is most effective when used as a surprise weapon. A batsman bowled by a yorker is said to be 'yorked'.

Z z

Zero Nil score by a batsman, whether out or not out. However, out for zero (or duck) is more notable and suggests total failure on the part of the batsman in the particular innings.

zooter A delivery that goes through straight after pitching, although bowled with a normal right-arm leg-spin action; more commonly referred to as the 'straighter 'un'. The delivery got its name from the great Australian leg-spinner, Shane Warne, who bowled it with good effect in the Ashes series of 1994–95 and called it the 'zooter'.